NOTTINGHAMSHIRE

1. *Frontispiece. Early Norman nave, Blyth Priory Church*

ROY CHRISTIAN

NOTTINGHAMSHIRE

B. T. Batsford Ltd
London

First published 1974

© Roy Christian 1974

ISBN 0 7134 2764 7

Printed and bound in Great Britain by
William Clowes & Sons Limited,
London, Colchester and Beccles
for the publishers B. T. Batsford Ltd,
4 Fitzhardinge Street, London W1H 0AH

CONTENTS

ACKNOWLEDGMENTS

The Author and Publishers would like to thank the following for permission to use photographs in this book: Barnaby's Picture Library (Pl. 30); J. Allan Cash (Pls. 12–15, 17, 19–22, 25–28, 31–34, 36); A. F. Kersting (Pls. 3, 6, 8–11, 16, 18, 23, 24, 29, 35, 37); National Building Record (Pls. 1, 7); Kenneth Scowen (Pls. 2, 4, 5). The map of Nottinghamshire is by courtesy of Patrick Leeson.

The Author would like to thank the Editor of *Country Life* for permission to use some material which has appeared there in a different form.

LIST OF ILLUSTRATIONS

NOTTINGHAMSHIRE

YORKSHIRE

DERBYSHIRE

LINCOLNSHIRE

LEICS.

Finningley

Idle

Trent

Stockwith

Scrooby

Everton

Gringley
on the Hill

Mattersey

Clayworth

Blyth

Barnby Moor

Wheatley

Hayton

Carlton
in Lindrick

Sturton le Steeple

Littleborough

Ranby

Clarborough

North Leverton
with Habblesthorpe

Worksop

Babworth

East Retford

South Leverton

Treswell

Rampton

Clumber Park

Laneham

Welbeck
Abbey

Carburton

Bothamsall

Dunham

Newton on Trent

Norton

East Markham

Cuckney

Thoresby

West Markham

Harby

Meden

Tuxford

Egmanton

Edwinstowe

Laxton

Ollerton

Ossington

Maun

Clipstone

Carlton on Trent

Teversal

Mansfield

Eakring

Cromwell

Collingham

Maplebeck

Holme

Sutton
in Ashfield

North Muskham

Kirkby
in Ashfield

Blidworth

Farnsfield

Kelham

Halam

Averham

Newark
on Trent

Annesley
Woodhouse

Newstead

Southwell

Halloughton

Fiskerton

Hawton

Balderton

Linby

Papplewick

Cxton

Calverton

Epperstone

Thurgarton

Elston

Woodborough

Gonalston

Trent

Devon

Eastwood

Lambley

Lowdham

Hoveringham

Cossall

Gunthorpe

East Bridgford

NOTTINGHAM

Shelford

Car Colston

Scarrington

Orston

Aslockton

Bramcote

Radcliffe on Trent

Bingham

Elton

Stapleford

Beeston

Cropwell Butler

Granby

Attenborough

Cotgrave

Cropwell Bishop

Langar

Ruddington

Owthorpe

Calston Bassett

Thrumpton

Kinoulton

Bunny

Kingston on Soar

Widmerpool

West Leake

Wysall

Willoughby
on the Wolds

Upper Broughton

Sutton Bonington

East Leake

Rempstone

(Vernemetum)

Normanton on Soar

Soar

Trent

0   5   10
miles

CHAPTER ONE

Introduction

If you drive northward along the M1 your introduction to Nottinghamshire is a road sign warning you of low-flying aircraft, followed almost immediately by another sign suggesting that you may encounter deer crossing the road over the next three miles. Although the chances of your actually meeting either of these hazards is remote, the fact that the signs are there at all suggests that you are entering a county of character. Their juxtaposition is somehow symbolic of a county where modern technology and an ancient rural past are sometimes separated by no more than the width of a hedge.

A good deal of evidence can be summoned to support this statement. There are places in Nottinghamshire where you can be lost in dense woodland within three minutes of passing a modern colliery. There are few more remote and romantic spots than D. H. Lawrence's 'Strelley Mill', but there is a coal mine less than a mile away. Few other counties can show a visitor a cathedral in what is virtually a village, factories built to look like castles, a village where farming is still carried out on the pre-enclosure open field system, or oil wells in cornfields. Nottinghamshire has all these, and many other oddities. In a county where the unconventional is almost commonplace it is hardly surprising that its most famous inhabitant may never have existed and was probably not a Nottinghamshire native even if he did.

A great deal of research—some scholarly, some slightly dotty—has been done on Robin Hood without conclusively proving who he was or when he lived, if at all. I have neither the qualifications nor the ambition to add any new thoughts on this old topic. You are perfectly free to decide for yourself whether he was a late-thirteenth century Robert Hood of Wakefield, a slightly earlier thirteenth-century outlaw of the same name, a slightly later Robyn Hode, or a purely mythical figure from the pagan past. My only advice is not to voice dogmatic scepticism in Nottinghamshire. He is, after all, the county's greatest tourist attraction. It is the places associated with Robin Hood: Nottingham Castle and the Dukeries, that the visitor wants to see; the rest of the county he is apt to dismiss as dull.

This is too harsh a view. 'It isn't a dramatic county, but it's a very pleasant one', said the lady I found painting in Owthorpe churchyard, putting my own thoughts into words. It has none of the spectacular scenery of gritstone edges and limestone dales of its western and northern neighbours, Derbyshire and Yorkshire. It is a county of gentler, rolling landscapes, more closely akin to those of Lincolnshire and Leicestershire to the south and east. If its highest point does not reach 7oo feet, it is rarely flat and monotonous. Nobody would claim it to be the most beautiful of English counties; nor the ugliest. In fact it is hardly the 'most' anything. It is a county in which one uses superlatives sparingly; a county in which everything is on a small scale, whether it be attractive views, industrial belts or subtopian villadom. Nottinghamshire has all these, often mixed together within a space of a few miles.

There is indeed one view of a very small portion of Nottinghamshire that seems to me to take in most of the main features of the county at a glance, but with odd perversity you have to go outside the county to see it. If you stand on the Derbyshire side of the Trent at Trent Lock, you look almost straight across at the mouth of the River Soar, which here separates Nottinghamshire from Leicestershire. Your first view of Nottinghamshire reveals a railway bridge carrying the main line from Derby and Nottingham across the Trent. The line burrows through a castellated entrance of a tunnel in a thickly wooded red-soiled hillside beyond which rise the cooling towers and chimneys of a new electric power station. There, in a flash, Nottinghamshire is symbolically represented to you: the Trent, communications, red soil, woodlands, the touch of eccentric grandeur at the tunnel mouth, the power station.

To understand Nottinghamshire's history you must know about the river and the forest. The Trent brought people into the county: Sherwood Forest kept them out. That may sound paradoxical, but it is broadly true. Most early invaders came into what is now Nottinghamshire along the Trent or its valley, but finding the thick woodland and undergrowth unfavourable for settlement, usually pressed on westwards. Some stayed, of course, on gravel terraces above the river, but only a few families settled near the forest or the heavy clay lands.

This early pattern of settlement remained curiously fossilized until the encroachment of the Forest from south and west began a century ago. About a million people live today on just over half a million acres, which makes it sound a fairly average county. Yet it is in fact curiously lop-sided. Roughly half its population lives in what can be loosely called the 'greater Nottingham area' in the south-west, with another quarter tightly packed up the west and north-west side around Mansfield and Worksop. The remaining 200,000 or so are thinly scattered across much more than half the area of the county.

This imbalance, as I have already suggested, is largely caused by geological factors. I am no geologist, but fortunately the geological structure of the county in very broad general terms can be fairly easily explained. The oldest rocks lie up the west side. Here are the coal measures, the eastern edge of the Derbyshire coalfield with some magnesian limestone, especially farther north. East of Worksop and Mansfield, and stretching right down to the city of Nottingham, is the Bunter sandstone, which one tends to think of as the characteristic rock of the county. Running north-eastwards from Mapperley Plains, on the north-eastern outskirts of Nottingham, are the Keuper sandstones, giving rise to higher ground to the west of the alluvial valley of the Trent, which is nearly two miles wide in places, and intermingling with the wider belts of Lias clays and red marls that occupy much of the east of the county.

This geological pattern, more complicated than I have made it appear here, has influenced not only the county's history and pattern of settlement but also its appearance. Apart from the green of forest and grasslands, red is the predominant Nottinghamshire colour. The churches are usually of stone quarried within the county, with importations of oolitic limestone from Ancaster, just across the Lincolnshire border, for a few specially lavish buildings, but secular stone buildings are comparatively rare outside the towns, and predominantly stone built villages rarer still. Nor, more surprisingly, is the county rich in half-timbering, except again, in a few towns and a handful of villages in the extreme south west in the valleys of the Soar and Trent. So Nottinghamshire is largely a county of red brick towns and villages. This sounds dull and often is in the west of the county where the bricks wear a particularly drab shade that the Welsh slate roofs fittingly cap with the correct funeral note. But over much of the county especially away from the industrial areas, the brickwork becomes lighter and more cheerful to blend well with the county's characteristic red pantiled roofs. On the sort of grey Midland day that Belloc thought typical these all-red roofs can appear monotonous, but in a strong light against a blue sky they have a gaiety and charm that is irresistible.

This is particularly true of the villages of the Keuper marl country that sometimes sit boldly along green ridges or nestle in hollows among the cornfields, and even more perhaps of those in the clay lands, where the wide horizons and clear light remind you that East Anglia and the Low Countries are not far away. The Bunter sandstone has few ancient villages because, as in the limestone uplands of Derbyshire and the chalk downs of the south, the soil is thin and there is little surface water. Rain quickly seeps through the porous rock to a water table that has always been deep lying and is sinking now as it is being increasingly tapped to slake the thirst of a rising population in the surrounding towns.

The Bunter is basically the legendary Sherwood Forest. It originally covered an area 25 miles long and 10 miles wide, stretching from the Trent between Gunthorpe and Wilford in the south to Worksop and the River Meden in the north; from the Leen valley in the west to the Dover Beck in the east. It was not exclusively dense forest. Like the New Forest, it had its stretches of open heathland with gorse, ling and broom, especially in the south. Further north there was thicker woodland of oak, birch and beech, some of which remains. Improved methods of cultivation opened up a good deal of the southern portion to agriculture centuries ago, but the north had only a few scattered settlements until well into the present century when the deep coal seams were tapped and new colliery villages sprang up at Ollerton, Bilsthorpe, Blidworth and elsewhere, relying for water on deep wells.

Nottinghamshire, therefore, has not proved a rewarding county for archaeologists. The exciting cave finds in the magnesian limestone at Cresswell Crags, astride the Derbyshire border, have been mainly in that county, and the most interesting exclusively Nottinghamshire discoveries have come as a result of gravel working in the Trent Valley

14

around Beeston and Attenborough and in the river itself. Two dug-out canoes were brought out of the Trent between Clifton and Wilford on the outskirts of Nottingham itself in 1938, and three more came to light at Holme Pierrepont in 1967. The Bronze Age has yielded few significant finds, but there are five known Iron Age sites, four of them fairly close together in the Keuper Marl country.

The Roman invasion has left one obvious mark on the face of the county. This is the Fosse Way, which cuts across the south-eastern wolds from Six Hills to Newark-on-Trent on its way from Axmouth to Lincoln. In the early period of Roman occupation the line of the road marked the effective northern limit of their conquest. Along it ran a string of forts. Four of these have been identified within the county. *Margidunum*, near East Bridgford, is the one that has been most closely studied by archaeologists. It covered an area of seven or eight acres, large enough for a garrison of 1,000 men. It is thought to have been sacked and burnt in A.D. 61, presumably by the Coritani, the Celtic people who inhabited most of what was to become Nottinghamshire, and then rebuilt. By the end of the first century it was no longer a military station but continued to be occupied as a settlement on the great road. There was a similar settlement at *Segelocum*, now Littleborough, on the west bank of the Trent, where a Roman link road, now called Till Bridge Lane, crossed the river by a stone-paved ford. Roman villas have been turned up at various places, but not in sufficient number to suggest that the county was thickly occupied. Certainly no Nottinghamshire town has a Roman origin, although Newark, on the Fosse Way, may have had a few houses.

Most of the evidence for Anglian and Saxon occupation lies in the place-names. A glance at a map is sufficient grounds for assuming that it was along the Trent that these people from north-west Europe came. Early Anglo-Saxon -*ington* and -*ingham* endings abound on both sides of the river. Walkeringham, Collingham, Hoveringham, Ruddington and Nottingham itself all lie within a mile of the Trent. From such early settlements, later settlers fanned out to build the numerous villages with simple -*ing*, -*ton*, -*ham* and -*worth* place-name endings, though such names are noticeably scarcer as one travels north. Here the streams become becks and most of the place-names are unmistakably Danish. There is a distinctive group in the west round Kirkby, Huthwaite and Skegby, and another a little farther to the north-east, within the forest, with the hamlets of Budby, Walesby, Thoresby, and Perlethorpe, not far from the Anglo-Saxon Ollerton and Boughton. Clearly this was border country as it had been earlier when it was claimed by the kingdoms of Northumbria and Mercia. Mercia finally won that border contest when Edwin defeated the Northumbrian army, probably at Eaton on the banks of the River Idle near Retford in 617. Shortly after this, Paulinus brought Christianity from York into Nottinghamshire, but his work was quickly destroyed when Penda became king of Mercia, and another 20 years were to pass before missionaries from Repton began a lasting conversion.

More than a century of comparative peace followed before the Danes harried and pillaged their way into Mercia, besieging the Anglian settlement of Snotingham. This later became the royal borough of Nottingham, one of the five main fortified trading centres of the Danelaw. It was the administrative centre for a section of the Danish army spread out over the surrounding countryside. Sometime before 1016 the territory thus occupied became Nottinghamshire, with boundaries that have barely changed since.

Its first seven centuries were relatively uneventful. The Battle of Stoke in 1487 was a postscript to the Wars of the Roses rather than the last battle in that squalid gang warfare, and the Civil War was little more than a protracted series of disturbances that added a few footnotes from Nottinghamshire to the pages of national history. It was only deep down in the Forest that something stirred during those centuries.

Sherwood Forest, the 'Shire Wood', may already, as tradition asserts, have been a hunting ground of Saxon and Danish kings before 1066. But it was the Normans who imposed the severe forest laws to protect the royal game, built a hunting lodge at Clipstone and established a pattern of administration to cover about a fifth of the county. The royal forest was divided into separate wards, each of which was supposed to hold a court every 42 days at Linby, Calverton, Mansfield and Edwinstowe. This was in addition to the swainmotes, assemblies of free forest tenants, that were held three times a year, the great Courts or Forest Eyres that met every seventh year, and the Regard, or Inspection of Boundaries, that was intended to carry out a survey once in three years. These courts may have met zealously in early times when Norman and Plantagenet kings regularly hunted the deer, but the records suggest a gradual slackening

2. (opposite, above) *Robin Hood's statue outside the gatehouse of Nottingham Castle*

3. (below) *Nottingham. The brick church of St Nicholas, dating from* 1678

of administration. Nor were the forest laws always rigidly enforced for much the same reason that it is impossible to ensure that every motorist keeps within the speed limit.

Much poaching went on. Not all of it was the work of outlaw bands of the Robin Hood variety. Villagers from the settlements that sprang up around the Forest and their lords, lay or monastic, were not above a day's or night's sport that would bring home the venison without significantly reducing the stock of deer. A census of 1531 recorded 4,280 red deer and 1,131 fallow deer within the Forest.

It was Henry VIII who ordered the census, but like the rest of the Tudors he had only a minimal interest in the Forest, or in Nottinghamshire as a whole, even Elizabeth I finding no bed to sleep in within the county. The decline of the Forest began at much the same time as the suppression of the monasteries, though it was less sudden and less complete. Today some 40,000 acres of Nottinghamshire are under woodland, most of it within the bounds of Sherwood.

The remains of the once splendid religious houses are far less impressive, Newstead apart. Even the great Cluniac priory of Lenton is sunk within the city of Nottingham leaving scarcely a stone to see, save a wonderful Norman font now in Holy Trinity Church, Lenton. Monastic lands passed into private hands as elsewhere, and new mansions sprang up on the sites of the old monasteries. The families enriched in this way were joined by others whose wealth came from the backs of sheep or from the minerals of the earth.

The Industrial Revolution arrived early in Nottinghamshire. In the reign of Elizabeth I the Willoughbys had established an industrial empire around Wollaton, and in 1588 Sir Francis Willoughby completed the building there of a palace fit for a new kind of emperor. Just a year later and a few miles to the east at Calverton a clergyman named William Lee invented a machine that was to revolutionise the stocking-knitting industry. Less fortunate than Willoughby, he made no money from his inspiration that laid the foundation of an industry. Framework knitting became one of the staple industries of Nottinghamshire and it lived on into the present century. For Lee's monument you have to look not at a palace but at long windows in eighteenth-century cottages still scattered around the southern half of the county and to the history book accounts of the Luddite troubles of the early nineteenth century.

4. (opposite, above) *Trent Bridge, Nottingham*

5. (below) *Nottingham University, Trent Building*

This outbreak of unrest, which took the form mainly of machine breaking with some rick burning, was at its height between 1811 and 1817. It was the outcome of a period of falling wages, rising prices and unemployment, caused by the French war and the troubles, leading to war in 1812, with the United States. The rioters were called Luddites from their practice of sending threatening letters signed 'Ned Ludd' or 'King Ludd' to master hosiers who cut wages or sacked workers. The names are thought to derive from a Leicestershire stockinger's apprentice named Ned Ludlam who in a moment of frustration smashed up a machine with a hammer. But Ludlam had nothing to do with the riots, and if there ever was a 'master mind' behind them his name is still a secret. More likely there were many leaders, some undoubtedly men of considerable organising ability who were more than a match for the authorities. In defiance of 4,000 soldiers, hundreds of special constables and a hasty Act of Parliament to make frame smashing a capital offence, the Luddites destroyed 1,000 frames and 100 lace machines in the peak period between November 1811 and February 1812. Not until 1820 when trade began to improve were the hosiers and their machines safe from the Luddites.

Framework knitting rarely offered high financial rewards to its workers, but it was important in that its machines and skills provided a runway for the factory based hosiery and lace trades. It was chiefly because of the local expertise that the cotton industry began in Nottingham, where James Hargreaves and Richard Arkwright independently set up mills in 1768. Twenty years later there were 28 cotton mills in the county, but few of them survived for long, largely because of the lack of fast-flowing streams.

Ironically, it is Nottinghamshire water that now supplies much of the nation's power. Since the last war a chain of new electric power stations has been built along the Trent Valley from Staffordshire to Lincolnshire. Six of these stations, including some of the biggest in Europe, are in Nottinghamshire, close to the heart of England, and, equally important, close to the coalfields.

The most productive mines in the most productive coalfield in Britain lie within the county. While the coalmining industry has been shrinking nationally, new deep pits have been sunk to tap the hidden seams in east Nottinghamshire. The most modern, Bevercotes, is about

3,000 feet deep, so that a miner crouching at its coal face is almost as far below ground as the climber standing on the summit of Scafell is above sea level.

Coalmines and power stations are hardly the stuff of which tourism is made; features which are usually glossed over in books of this sort. But they cannot be ignored. A book about Nottinghamshire must include warts and all. And the warts are an integral part of the county's face. Admittedly they disfigure the face in places, but not the overall impression. Most of the new collieries are unobtrusive; freckles rather than warts. The older pits in the west are less satisfactory, though even here much has been done and is still being done to tidy up existing mines and scars left by disused ones. Much still remains to be done, however. 2,500 acres of derelict land, devastation caused by the greed of earlier industrialists, cannot be returned to agriculture or amenity use in a year or two.

About the power stations it is possible to have two opinions. Many people react strongly against their appearance. But I find that my own ideas, anyway, are changing. The voluptuous curves of cooling towers have an appeal. Even pylons in certain places have their attractions, though insensitively sited they can be dreadful. Some tangled masses of wires, pylons and towers do mar the serenity of the Trent Valley, but other power stations add a touch of drama to a river that had conspicuously lacked that quality.

Visitors are sometimes disappointed by the Trent. Too many expect to find the traditional boundary between north and south forming a definite topographical division between highland on one side and lowland on the other. Nothing of the sort happens. For much of its course through the county the river flows due north, anyway, and even where it does flow roughly east there is little feeling that one is crossing a frontier. There is nowhere in Nottinghamshire, as there is in neighbouring Derbyshire, where a southern visitor can sense that he has reached the north of England, any more than he can on the county's other important through line of communication, the Great North Road.

Yet there is in the character of its people a quirky quality that seems to have more in common with the north than the south. I am not thinking of such aristocratic eccentrics as the 'wicked Lord' Byron, with his folly forts and his naval engagements on the lake at

Introduction

Newstead, though the county has produced a good quota of these. I am thinking of less exalted people, and it would be possible to find among those who have played cricket for their county a number of excellent examples to make my point. Two must suffice. One must be George Gunn, a brilliant, unorthodox batsman, who would often predict to the fieldsmen within earshot the approximate number of runs he proposed to make in his innings. The prediction would vary quite widely according to the mood of the moment, which depended largely on the uncertain state of his health, and was usually remarkably accurate. Having reached his required quota, George would ask courteously, 'Which of you gentlemen would like a catch?', and having selected a suitable volunteer, would steer the next convenient delivery into the correct pair of hands.

After Gunn retired from cricket, at a fairly advanced age despite his poor health, Charlie Harris from Underwood settled into the side as a solid, outwardly orthodox opening batsman, whose batting gave less entertainment to the spectators than to his fellow players. His habit was to give a running commentary on his own innings in the style then favoured by the *Nottingham Evening Post*, in common with most other papers. 'Refusing to be intimidated by barracking', he would say, 'the Underwood professional settled down to play a typically dour innings, being at the wicket for 32 minutes before opening his account'. And so it went on. But not all Harris's humour was verbal. Once, convinced the light was unfit for further play, he borrowed a workman's lantern and came out to bat holding it aloft. The umpires took the hint; bad light stopped play.

I am not suggesting that all Nottinghamshire men are natural comics, or that life in the county is one long laugh, but I do detect a rich vein of slightly off-beat humour that D. H. Lawrence, otherwise a faultless depictor of Nottinghamshire character and speech, hardly noticed at all except in a few short stories. It is more pronounced amongst the miners on the west side of the county, and it takes the form of a sort of 'in' humour of semi-private jokes that act as a safety-valve for men whose lives are daily in danger. It is much like wartime Services humour; dry, laconic; delivered in terse, hammer-blow sentences with short, emphatic vowels which Richard Hoggart sees as the genesis of Lawrence's literary style.

Over the last half century those vowel sounds have had to compete

22

with very different accents of Durham and South Wales, as miners from those areas moved away to escape the worst effects of the Great Depression. More recent pit closures there have hastened the pace of immigration, chiefly to the new mines, where Lewises and Lilburns may find themselves working alongside local born miners whose names originated in Eastern Europe. In the city of Nottingham coloured workers and their families have added a further cosmopolitan touch to what has been for centuries a notably gay and vital city.

Nottingham's sparkle is not obviously reflected in the county's other towns, workaday places mainly of no great size or special historical and architectural interest, with two exceptions. Newark, in the heart of an agricultural area, makes up for the rest in charm and aesthetic interest, and Southwell is 'a country town with the over-powering presence of a large medieval church', in the words of Sir Nicholas Pevsner, whose work on Nottinghamshire, the first volume in the *Buildings of England* series has accompanied me on all my excursions into the county and has been constantly consulted.

Indeed there is a danger, with so knowledgeable a guide at hand, of producing a mere catalogue of churches, for although collectively the Nottinghamshire churches may not equal the magnificence of those of East Anglia, the Cotswolds or Somerset, there are excellent examples of churches from most centuries. The thirteenth and fourteenth centuries produced many good ones, the fifteenth century even more, which probably reflects the growing prosperity of the wool trade. But I have tried to avoid lingering too long in these churches, commenting only on those I found outstanding or unusual, and regretfully omitting others simply because of lack of space, or, in a very few cases, because I was unable to locate the key of a locked church. Keeping a church locked is understandable, unfortunately, but information about where to ask for the key would be helpful. Of course, I should add that this is a general complaint, not aimed at Nottinghamshire only.

Speaking of complaints, there may be some lifting of eyebrows that a Derbyshire man should dare to write about Nottinghamshire. My defence is that I was born so close a neighbour as almost to claim myself an honorary Nottinghamshire man. I was born a mere mile outside the county, and when for a time I went to school at Mansfield I crossed the boundary daily on my walk to the local L.M.S. station, now closed, like its Great Northern neighbour. From either station we could get a train direct to Nottingham; a journey to Derby involved a tedious change. So it was in Nottingham we shopped, in Nottingham I saw my earliest first class cricket and football, and in the *Nottingham Evening Post* that we read all about them, and all those fascinating filler paragraphs about Bulgarian centenarians who had just become fathers of twins. In the early years of the war my family lived in Nottinghamshire, and a little later I spent 13 months in the north of the county. All this puts me in the pleasant position of seeing the county as an outsider with reasonable inside knowledge, which gives me an affection for Nottinghamshire and the privilege extended to a member of a family—if a distant member—of offering occasional criticism without, I hope, causing offence.

I have assumed that most readers will see Nottinghamshire by car, but I have tried also to remember those sensible people who prefer to walk. Nottinghamshire is better walking country than you might think, unless you belong to the hardy Pennine Walk brigade. It has numerous fascinating bridle and foot paths, usually well signposted, though the occasional direction post that tersely indicates *Public Footpath*, and no more, hardly seems adequate.

I have also assumed that most people will use Nottingham as a base for exploring at least the southern half of the county, perhaps using Mansfield, the second largest town, or Worksop for the northern half. If they were not quite so far east, either Newark or Southwell would be most pleasant bases for explorations.

My own expeditions over the county in recent years have influenced my division of the county into its various sections. Each area can be explored in three or four hours—or three or four weeks—according to taste. And if the choice seems arbitrary it does in fact coincide fairly accurately with the geological divisions of what seems to me a most interesting county.

CHAPTER TWO

Nottingham

A Town of Improbable Splendours

Nottingham likes to be called 'Queen of the Midlands'. It is an apt title for a city as unmistakably feminine as Birmingham is undoubtedly masculine. Yet it is not easy to say how this quality of femininity has arisen. Certainly Nottingham's history, especially in political and industrial affairs, has often been most rough and unladylike. Partly it may lie in a certain elegance in its buildings that even recent development has not entirely obliterated; partly in the fact that much of its evident wealth springs from the manufacture of such essentially feminine goods as lace, hosiery and cosmetics; partly it may stem from the boast—possibly claimed by many another city—that it has the prettiest and best dressed girls in England. The sum of all these parts is a city of elegance and charm, capable certainly of a boisterousness, even coarseness of behaviour, but essentially feminine.

When I was a small boy, Nottingham was our nearest large shopping centre and seemed to me to be a glamorous, exciting and sometimes frightening city. Attractive, almost intimidatingly smartly dressed women carried parcels, bearing names like Griffin and Spalding, Jessop, or Dixon and Parker, or sat daintily sipping tea and munching hot buttered toast in tea-shops that looked out across the biggest market place in England. And just off the main shopping streets were dark alleyways where men unloaded strangely shaped parcels from horse-drawn drays and humped them into tall, dark Dickensian warehouses. But it is the noises I remember best; the clanging trams, the rumble of horse-drawn drays on cobbled streets, the tip-tap of high heels on pavements.

That was winter Nottingham. A city where Christmas was perpetually a mere fortnight away; a city where fog swirled incessantly round the gaunt warehouses and my mother, already over-laden with Christmas presents, began to talk nervously of catching an earlier train in case they stopped running.

But there was also a summer Nottingham. Arkwright Street, frowsty with heat even in mid-morning suddenly opening out at the approach to Trent Bridge, where the river sparkled in the sun and a fresh breeze tingled the blood. And then there were queues already forming outside the turnstiles of the Trent Bridge Cricket Ground and a dreadful fear that the ground might even then be full. This gave way to delirious happiness as the turnstiles clicked behind us and we were in time to see George Gunn and Whysall come out to face the bowling of Bill Hitch and Peach. Somehow, those two batsmen symbolize for me the two sides of Nottingham's character. Gunn, all elegance and grace, would not have been out of place in those Long Row tea-shops. Walter Whysall, cautious and orthodox, belonged to the Nottingham of office and warehouse. Almost invariably, it seems, when I watched them, Gunn made his 30 or 40 with stylish gaiety and then threw away his wicket with aristocratic abandon; Whysall plodded his way dourly through the long hot afternoon to make his pile of runs. Here indeed were the two faces of Nottingham.

These are subjective, nostalgic impressions. Yet, when you look objectively at Nottingham's history you find that for many centuries it really did wear two faces. The modern city is the progeny of the marriage of two quite separate boroughs.

If you stand in the vast old market place—and there is nearly six acres of it, including the Council House block—you can best take in the development of early Nottingham. On three sides the streets slope gently upwards; on the fourth there is a still more gradual slope downwards towards the Trent, a mile or so away. The eastern and western slopes are the ones to notice first. It was on the soft sandstone hill behind the modern Council House that the original Anglian settlement of Snotingham, the homestead of Snotingas— followers of Snot, an Anglian leader—was established about A.D. 500 on land that had already been sporadically occupied from Neolithic times. The rectangular site, on St. Mary's Hill, covered about 39 acres, one side having the natural defence of a low cliff above the marshes. Protection on the other three sides was eventually provided by a ditch and bank.

Nothing of the first three centuries of Snotingham's history is known; nothing in fact before 868 when 'the heathen host left the

Northumbrians and came with dreadfulness to Snotingham'. These heathen were the Vikings, led by the splendidly named Halfdan and Ivar the Boneless, sons of the notorious Ragnar Lothbrook. To resist this invasion the King of Mercia, Burhed, sent for his brothers-in-law, Ethelred, King of Wessex, and Alfred, then a young man of 19, who promptly 'came unto Snotingham ready to face the fray'. There was, it seems, no fray. Peace terms were arranged and both armies retired without raising a battleaxe in anger. But soon the Danes returned, and in due course Nottingham became one of their five royal boroughs. fortified trading centres of the Danelaw, along with Derby, Leicester, Lincoln and Stamford.

So much then for St. Mary's Hill, so called from its church which occupies a central position in the old 'English' borough. We should look westward now to the 'French' borough, and it is worth mentioning here that the distinction was clearly made until the fifteenth century; that two sheriffs and two coroners were elected until 1835, and that two maces are still carried in procession before the Sheriff of Nottingham. The French borough was an appendage of the castle, a Norman settlement that clustered for protection against the castle walls and then spilled eastward down the hill in a series of streets that survive today, such as Mount Street, St. James's Street, Friar Lane, Hounds Gate and Castle Gate. The old market place may have originated as a stretch of 'no man's land' between the two boroughs, but later it was certainly embraced within the 80 acres of the Norman borough, though by the twelfth century it had become a common market place for both communities. It was, however, divided by a wall which survived at least into the seventeenth century. It used to be accepted that this was to separate the English and French communities and prevent fighting. Later historians have doubts, suggesting that the wall merely separated the livestock from the other goods. They may be right, but I have a sneaking preference for the older theory.

In spirit, the old market place still seems to separate the two boroughs. As a generalization it is fair to say that the modern shopping and entertainment centre, including the Playhouse, Theatre Royal and the cinemas, lie within the French borough; the old commercial and professional centre stands in the jumble of narrow streets in the restricted confines of the English borough. In atmosphere they remain entities; as though ancient national characteristics have somehow become fossilized. Eastward, on St. Mary's Hill, life seems to be devoted to work and piety; westward, in the modern city centre, it is given up to pleasure and gaiety. Is it too fanciful to suggest that the main clue to the sparkling feminine quality of Nottingham may lie in that long forgotten French ancestry which has somehow carried a few of its genes into the twentieth century?

Today the old market place has become Old Market Square; dubbed 'Slab Square', scornfully, by some older Nottinghamians who feel that concrete paving stones are poor substitutes for the colourful stalls that used to brighten the city centre before the covered market in Huntingdon Street was opened in 1928, and regret the removal of the famous Goose Fair to the Forest in that same year. Visitors to Nottingham, on the other hand, are usually impressed by this great open space—nearly three quarters of a mile in circumference—at the city's heart, though they may not unanimously approve of the massively domed Council House that was opened by the then Prince of Wales on 22 May 1929. 'Not much can be said in defence of this kind of neo-Baroque display', in Pevsner's view, but in 1968 *The Times* obituarist of the building's architect, the Nottingham-born T. Cecil Howett, acclaimed it 'probably still the finest municipal building outside London'. Most people enjoy its central shopping arcade with historical frescoes by the local artist Denholm Davis, and the figures on the façade by Joseph Else, then principal of the Nottingham art school. I must say that I rather like the building, though I have felt less enthusiasm for the booming of its great clock— Little John—when I have tried to sleep within its considerable sound-range. The Old Market Square must be one of the wonders of modern Nottingham, but it is the Castle that most visitors seek out first.

Its position is superb; its architecture ludicrous. But astonishingly in what is basically an industrial and commercial centre, Nottingham Castle is England's most popular tourist attraction outside London. In 1971 it welcomed 532,000 visitors, some, no doubt, just to bask in its gardens, others to view its excellent museum and art gallery, many more attracted by the legend of Robin Hood. Sitting squarely on the flat top of a spectacular red sandstone rock, Nottingham Castle is the victim of its own virtues and of the accidents of history. Its position, almost as noble as that of Edinburgh Castle or Bamburgh Castle, demands to be crowned by as noble a pile, or at least by some impressive ruin like Tantallon or Chepstow; not by what looks like a couple of pill-boxes side by side.

The trouble is that Nottingham Castle is not a true castle at all; it is a baroque mansion of the late seventeenth century that was restored two centuries later to fit it for a new life as the first municipal museum in England. For either of these latter purposes it would look well enough if it stood in private parkland, especially since its outer coating of grime has been removed, but for the romantically minded visitor hoping for battlements fit for Robin Hood to escape from, it is something of an anti-climax. To make matters worse, there is nothing within the Castle to link it with the outlaw, though just below its walls there is his splendidly lively modern statue by James Woodford.

Having been slightly disparaging about Nottingham Castle, I must make amends by saying that for all its imperfections it is dearly loved by Nottingham people—and by me. It has indeed a most interesting history, which can only be briefly sketched here. The first building on the site was almost certainly of the motte-and-bailey type with a wooden keep. It was built by order of William the Conqueror in 1068. One of his followers, William Peverel, became the first constable of the royal castle. A stone keep replaced the wooden one in the twelfth century and further improvements were carried out under successive kings until it reached its greatest splendour in the reign of Edward IV (1461–1483). As a royal house it was used frequently by reigning monarchs. As Nottinghamshire's earliest local historian, Dr Robert Thoroton, put it: 'Neither is there any place anything near so far distant from London that I know of in all England, which hath so often given intertainment and residence to the Kings and Queens of this realm since the Norman Conquest'. Among them were Richard III, who rode out from Nottingham to Bosworth and death in 1485, and Henry VII, who two years later slept there on the eve of the battle at East Stoke. But this visit apart, the Tudors seem to have cold-shouldered Nottingham Castle. In the reign of Henry VIII, John Leland found it ruinous but reparable. But the Earl of Rutland, who took it off the hands of James I, chose to demolish portions and sell the stones rather than repair. In 1643 Charles I preferred to sleep at Thurland Hall, in the town. By the time Thoroton wrote his words in 1677 the splendours of the castle had all perished, so that, as Celia Fiennes put it so quaintly 15 years later, '. . . only the ruinated walls remaine'.

The Civil War could, I suppose, be described as Nottingham Castle's 'finest hour'. It was there—not in the grounds but in 'a field a little on the back side of the Castle walls', to quote from a contemporary account—that Charles 1 raised his standard to start the war on 22 August 1642. For the King it proved a disappointing non-event. Of the 2,000 or so spectators, a mere 30 stayed behind to enlist. According to one account, the Standard symbolically blew down and was accidentally trampled in the mud. Certainly Charles was displeased. On the two following days the Standard was again raised, but with less ceremony as there were fewer spectators and even less support. Nottingham people, having kept out of trouble for the previous thousand years were not disposed to look for it then. In any event, their sympathies were probably more with Parliament, as was the case with most commercial centres. On 13 September the King, after further abortive negotiations with Parliament, marched away to Shrewsbury, his army strengthened by less than 300 recruits. The spot where the Standard flew lies close by Nottingham General Hospital, just off the street called Standard Hill.

Nottingham townsfolk then settled back to their own affairs and hoped that the war would just go away. But in December it came to the shire when a small force of local Royalists seized Newark and proposed to take Nottingham. But the townsfolk, in the words of Mrs Lucy Hutchinson, 'cared not much to have cavalier soldiers quarter with them, and therefore agreed to defend themselves against any force which should come against them'. There was a hasty meeting, 'about seven hundred listed themselves, and chose Mr George Hutchinson for their captain, who, having lived among them, was very much loved and esteemed by them'. This show of force was sufficient to deter the Royalists. By the time the threat was renewed in the following summer the Parliamentary forces in Nottingham were commanded by George Hutchinson's brother, Colonel John Hutchinson of Owthorpe, whose wife was to produce what has been aptly called 'the most valuable biographical work to come out of the whole period', *Memoirs of the Life of Colonel Hutchinson*.

Colonel Hutchinson did not have an easy war. His friends in the town were nearly as much trouble as his enemies outside. When, on assuming command, he withdrew his garrison of 400 men into the Castle and left the town to fend for itself, the inhabitants were naturally annoyed. Yet the decision was militarily sound. The town could not be defended by so small a force, whereas the Castle, protected on the outer side by a sheer rock falling 130 feet to the River Leen and on the inner by a steep slope down to a dry moat, was practically impregnable.

Three times the Royalists entered the town. The first occasion was in September, 1643, when a force of 600 Cavaliers from Newark, commanded by Sir Richard Byron, slipped in during the night—with the alleged complicity of Alderman Frank Toplady who commanded the watch—and took prisoner many of the Castle garrison who were sleeping at home in defiance of orders. For five days the Castle was besieged. Royalist snipers used the steeple of St. Nicholas's Church to make 'the outward Castle yard' virtually untenable. When the garrison was relieved by reinforcements from Leicester and Derby, Hutchinson had the church destroyed. In the following January, the Royalists from Newark returned with a larger force and managed to occupy the houses facing the Castle, from which a fierce counter attack forced them to retreat, and 'for two miles they left a great track of blood, which froze as it fell upon the snow'. But a month later a final attempt was made on the town. This time, however, Royalist security was faulty and Hutchinson was prepared. His men surprised 12 soldiers on Trent Bridge, 'disguised like market men and women, with pistols, long knives, hatchets, daggers and great pieces of iron about them', whereupon the main force hurriedly withdrew, though five who were ahead of the rest were drowned in trying to escape and five more were taken prisoner.

The end of the Civil War saw the end of Nottingham Castle's long history as a military stronghold. In common with most other fortified houses it was demolished, though the demolition order was obtained in 1651 not by Cromwell but by Hutchinson, for fear, his wife tells us, of 'Cromwell's poisonous ambition'. The stones were sold for use in buildings and roadwork in the town. The shell returned to the Earl of Rutland's estate, now represented by the Duke of Buckingham, who sold it in 1674 to the Duke of Newcastle, an ironical touch as Newcastle, when a noted Royalist cavalry leader in the Civil War, had been a constant source of worry to Hutchinson. The Duke probably took some satisfaction in razing what was left of the Castle and starting to build the present house at a cost of £14,000. Why a man of 82, who had lost almost one million pounds as a result of the Civil War, should want to build a lavish new house is a mystery which can only be explained by hereditary. He had building in his blood, being a grandson of the 'building Countess' Bess of Hardwick.

The Duke died in 1676, and his son completed the house three years later, but his successors spurned it. Gradually the Castle ceased to play an important part in the life of the town. The deer went from the park and were replaced by soldiers for whom a barracks was built. But they in turn were banished to Derby when the Corporation successfully petitioned that their presence was prejudicial to the morals of the town. By the beginning of the nineteenth century part of the Castle was let to favoured tenants, part housed a boarding school for young ladies and another portion was used as an armoury for the militia. It was thus a somewhat forlorn hotch-potch of a house which the Reform Bill rioters burnt down on the evening of 10 October 1831.

This incident took place on the third and most successful evening of the riots which followed the rejection of the Reform Bill by the House of Lords. On the Saturday evening when the news reached Nottingham, already crowded with visitors to the Goose Fair, the rioters indulged themselves in mere window breaking around the town, with a repeat performance on the Sunday, despite the reading of the Riot Act and the assembling of troops. On the Monday they became more ambitious. They destroyed a mill on the Forest and set fire, rather ineffectively, to Colwick Hall. Then, returning to the town centre, they split into two groups. One group went to the House of Correction where they failed in an attempt to release the prisoners. The other group, more enthusiastically, forced a passage into the Castle, ransacked and fired it, and then enterprisingly cut up the stolen tapestries into squares, selling them at three shillings a yard among the large crowd that had gathered despite pouring rain, to watch the blaze. Rioting continued next day, but by the evening order was restored and all was over but the hanging, for which, in due course, three victims were somewhat arbitrarily chosen.

The other result of the fire was that the fourth Duke of Newcastle, a vehement opponent of Reform, rather ungraciously accepted £21,000 in compensation paid with even less grace by the unfortunate inhabitants of the Hundred of Broxtowe, as the Castle at that time still lay outside the town boundary. But the Duke did nothing to restore the mansion. It stood for 40 years 'a stark and neglected ruin', until the Corporation took it over in 1875 on a 500-year lease—they bought it outright in 1952—and rebuilt it as a museum and art gallery, which was opened to the public by King Edward vii and Queen Alexandra (then Prince and Princess of Wales) in 1878.

Of the medieval Castle little remains but the gatehouse, and even that was greatly restored in 1908. And there are the underground passages in the rock—Nottingham is honeycombed by caves, some of them inhabited within living memory—through which parties of visitors are shown. The best known of these passages is Mortimer's Hole, traditionally, though evidence is thin, the one through which in 1330 some two dozen armed conspirators, led by William de Montacute (later first Earl of Salisbury), entered the Castle. They captured Roger, Earl of Mortimer, the lover of Queen Isabella, widow of the murdered Edward ii and mother of Edward iii. The young king was in the Castle at the time—and involved in the plot. Mortimer was later executed at Tyburn, despite the Queen's entreaty: 'Fair son, have pity on the gentle Mortimer'.

Mortimer's Hole is no place for the aged and infirm, and others are advised to see it after lunch, the mornings being usually reserved for school parties. The rest of the Castle and its grounds are open daily. The museum has interesting displays of medieval alabaster carvings, for which Nottingham was once famous, textiles, naturally enough, and now houses the Regimental Museum of the Sherwood Foresters. The art gallery specializes, though not exclusively, in local landscapes and the works of local artists. The brothers Paul (1725–1809) and Thomas (1721–98) Sandby, Richard Parkes Bonington (1802–1828), Sir John Alfred Arnesby Brown (1866–1955) and Dame Laura Knight (1877–1970) are all strongly represented. The landscapes from the seventeenth and eighteenth centuries confirm Defoe's opinion that Nottingham was then 'one of the most pleasant and beautiful towns in England'. But it was a town poised on the brink of changes that the Industrial Revolution was to bring.

In Defoe's time the population was barely 10,000: it grew to 25,000 by 1793 and 52,000 by 1841, almost wholly contained within the confines of the medieval town. Before the Nottingham Enclosure Act of 1845, all attempts to extend the town were blocked, according to

Professor J. D. Chambers, by the Duke of Newcastle and other noble landowners, and by the freemen of the town, who had grazing rights on the ancient common fields. Although this theory has now been challenged, the fact remains that on what had been described as an 'exquisite spot to build a town' was crammed 'a chequerboard of mean streets, alleyways and courts, and a byword for filth and misery beyond belief'. It became one of the most overcrowded towns in England. In 1844 in one area less than 220 yards square 4,200 people existed with just over ten square yards each that they could call their own. Not surprisingly the mean age of death in Nottingham in 1845, 22.3 years, was seven years lower than the national average. In one sub-district of St Ann's Ward the expectation of life was 11.1 years: the average of the whole Ward 18.1.

Fifty years ago it was still possible to look down from the Castle rock on to this 'resurrection of buildings, generally without order, seated like clusters of mushrooms in a field cast up by change'. Now most of them have gone, though there are still devastated areas where the former 'rookeries' await replacement by nobler buildings. But the view from Castle rock is now almost—if you forget the clutter of railway sidings and warehouses in the immediate south foreground—as fine as when Celia Fiennes in 1697 admired 'a very fine prospect of the whole town and river'.

Under the lee of the Castle on the west side is an extraordinary village within the city. This is a private housing estate of 155 acres within the old Castle park, planned by the fifth Duke of Newcastle in 1851 to provide peace and seclusion to the lace barons and other prosperous entrepreneurs of Nottingham. The scheme was designed by a local architect named Thomas Hine in a series of circuses, crescents and drives whose drawing-board symmetry is obscured by the uneven configuration of the land. In all, some 650 houses were built between 1854 and 1887—many of the largest by Hine himself and his assistant C. I. Evans—in a variety of styles, which, in the words of Professor A. C. Wood, represented the 'transition from disciplined Georgian to variegated villadom'. The Park was completely cut off from the rest of Nottingham by gates across the roads and a tunnel large enough for a railway tunnel that cut under the Rope Walk and barred the entrance from Derby Road to all except residents with keys.

Today the Park may not be quite what it was. Some of the larger houses have been demolished and replaced by new ones. Ownership of the estate has passed from the Newcastle interests to Oxford University, but many residents now own their own freehold. The tunnel was boarded up in 1962. But to enter the Park is still to enter another, more gracious world. When you pass through the white gate that leads from the Castle—flanked by speed restriction signs and notices barring coaches and parkers—you drop steeply down on a narrow private road cut through the solid rock into a hollow where the roar of Nottingham's traffic suddenly fades to silence. When you emerge again into the roar of Castle Boulevard the sheer side of the Castle rock looms ominously above you; particularly ominously on my last visit when tall scaffolding was being erected against the rock face ready for work to begin on a stabilization scheme. The house opposite is no doubt safe enough, but all the same I should not feel too happy about living there.

From Castle Boulevard a left turn brings you back into Castle Road, off which lies Brewhouse Yard, containing a few seventeenth-century houses and the Trip to Jerusalem Inn. The Trip carries the date 1189, reputedly acquired its name from its popularity with returning Crusaders whose throats were parched with the dust of the Holy Land, and claims to be the oldest pub in England. All three points could hardly be mooter, as P. G. Wodehouse might say, but for all that the Trip is worth a visit. It is genuinely medieval, with cellars cut into the Castle rock, and was probably the Castle brewhouse. But there are several other interesting old inns around the city centre; among them the Salutation, which is also medieval and again with rock cellars like so many Nottingham pubs; the Flying Horse, much restored but dating from around 1600, and the Bell in Angel Row.

Just above the Trip and facing the Robin Hood statue is Castle Gate. Its upper end has been turned into a charming pedestrian precinct. On one side a group of eighteenth-century houses has been restored by the City Architect's Department which now uses the block as offices. Opposite is Newdigate House, to my mind the most attractive house in Nottingham, though a massive new building in flaring red brick strikes a jarring note when you face it from the other side of Castle Gate. Newdigate House dates from about 1675 and, as

35

Pevsner says, 'displays stately alternating window pediments and some of the best ironwork railings and gates in Nottingham'. It was for seven years the prison—and the word could hardly be used more loosely—of Marshal Tallard, as a plaque on the wall proclaims.

The Duc de Tallard, who is still recalled affectionately if a little vaguely in Nottingham, commanded the unsuccessful French army at the Battle of Blenheim in 1704. He was a dashing, brave and generally able, if somewhat reckless, leader. At Blenheim, despite a slight numerical superiority, he allowed himself to be out-generalled by the Duke of Marlborough and was careless enough to get himself taken prisoner at the height of the battle, which does at least prove him to have been no back-room leader.

At Blenheim Palace in Oxfordshire you can see in a magnificent tapestry a representation of the meeting on the battlefield of Tallard and Marlborough. It is an excellent likeness of Tallard and shows him as an elegant, handsome little man—a youthful 52—and you can understand his subsequent popularity with the ladies of Nottingham. But first he was brought over to London with other important prisoners and kept there for six months before the Government decided that Nottingham afforded less chance of excape. There, in February 1705, he arrived with 12 other French noblemen after a leisurely journey broken by numerous comfortable inns—that is said to have cost the country over £2,000. He—or the British taxpayer—paid 50 shillings a week to the Colley family to rent their delightful modern house and gave some return for the money by laying out a magnificent garden at the back of the house which can still be seen in old plans of the town. It has been said that he introduced celery into this country. This may not be strictly true. Wild celery, it seems, already grew at Lenton and other places in the Nottingham area. But it is a fact that cultivated celery appeared on the Englishman's table around this time and it is likely that Tallard was a pioneer cultivator. Another useful service that tradition attributes to him was the instruction of local bakers in the art of making French rolls, and if their early efforts were slightly indigestible they were doubtless helped down by the vast quantities of champagne and burgundy that he received from London. They were sent to him by coach by Thomas Coke, Queen Anne's Vice-Chamberlain, probably, again, at the nation's expense.

Tallard and Coke were great friends, sharing a common interest in

6. (opposite, above) *Wollaton Hall, built* 1580–88

7. (below) *Victorian Gothic industrial architecture. Anglo-Scotian Mills, Beeston*

gardens and gracious living. Coke had just laid out the French-style gardens at Melbourne Hall in Derbyshire, which can be seen very little altered today, and Tallard was often there to admire them and offer friendly advice. Indeed he seems to have strayed well outside the ten mile radius of Nottingham to which he was nominally restricted, complimenting the Earl of Chesterfield on his gardens at Bretby and the Duke of Devonshire on owning 'the finest palace in the world' at Chatsworth, a handsome tribute from a man who knew Versailles. His smooth, sometimes witty tongue and polished manners made him a popular figure in the stately homes of the East Midlands, and there was general regret when his spell of 'captivity' ended in 1712 and he returned to France, leaving behind him pleasant memories that linger to this day, as well as—if contemporary gossip was true—visible mementos of his stay in Nottingham.

Maid Marian Way now bisects Castle Gate and must cover part of the site of Tallard's garden. 'One of the ugliest streets in Europe'; so Nottingham University's Professor of Architecture described this latest section of the town's inner ring-road in 1965, but the claim must be attributed to excessive local patriotism; Maid Marian Way is no worse, but little better, than countless other new roads that are tearing out the hearts of our cities. In fact it has not quite struck at the heart of Nottingham, though it caused the demolition of the Collin's Almshouses, rightly acclaimed by Pevsner, 'A lovely group, one of the best almshouses of its date [1709] in England'. This was deplorable, but as a minor compensation the new road has opened up a pleasing view of St Nicholas's Church. Even so, it is easy to disregard this fine church in its leafy churchyard; at a distance its warm red brick suggests a modern product. In fact it dates from 1678, 35 years after Hutchinson destroyed its predecessor, with aisles added about a century later and separated from the nave by white Tuscan pillars. It is a light, cheerful church with a good late-eighteenth century communion rail and an inlaid pulpit that dates from about the time the north aisle was completed in the 1780s.

The lower end of Castle Gate, where D. H. Lawrence worked as a boy in Hayward's surgical-appliance factory, has several notable Georgian houses. The most impressive is Stanford House, successively the home of wealthy lace and cotton manufacturers and not, as local mythology asserts, the town house of the Earls Howe, of Langar. This

8. & 9. (opposite) *Strelley family monuments in Strelley Church. The lower picture shows Sir Sampson de Strelley, who built the church in* 1356, *holding the hand of his wife, who died in* 1405

area west of the Castle and stretching towards St Mary's Church was the fashionable quarter of Nottingham in the eighteenth century. Castle Gate, despite being so rudely interrupted by Maid Marian Way, is probably still, as Pevsner said, 'the best street in Nottingham', but there are other fine town houses in St James's Street, including No. 76, where Byron stayed in 1798–9, and Low Pavement, with Willoughby House presenting an especially felicitous picture of early Georgian building in red brick beyond a fine wrought-iron gateway. Just north of this area, but worth the short detour, is Bromley House in Angel Row on the edge of Old Market Square. This 'very civilized' house, to quote Pevsner again, was built in 1752 for Sir George Smith, the banker. Since 1816 its first floor has housed the Nottingham Subscription Library, which is why its doorway is open by day, offering a fine view of a magnificent hall and staircase.

From here we should return to Low Pavement, which leads, reasonably enough, to High Pavement and to the narrow streets of the English borough: Weekday Cross, where a daily market survived from pre-Conquest times into the nineteenth century, Woolpack Lane, Warser Gate, Fletcher Gate—the 'Gates' deriving from the Norse *gata* (or Danish *gade*) 'a street'—Byard Lane, Stoney Street (Stanesstete in 1218) and Hollow Stone, originally just a gap in the rock. Here, among these evocatively named streets, are other buildings worth at least a second glance. Two of the more interesting face one another across High Pavement. On the north side is the former Judges Lodgings, originally a private house of around 1730 extended and embellished in 1833, when the cast-iron columns were put in to support a new dining room. Today the building is the County Records Office. Exhibitions of old documents are frequently held, to which the public have free admission during normal working hours. Opposite is the Shire Hall, a unique county enclave within the city—before local government reorganization. Its centre block, on the heavy side but not unpleasing (especially the Ionic portico), was built in 1770 by James Gandon, who is less well known in England than in Ireland, where he designed the Custom House and other buildings in Dublin. The flanking extensions were added about a century later in the Italianate style of the period.

Following the gentle, graceful curve of High Pavement, you come now, quite unexpectedly, to St Mary's Church, its tower curiously obscured at close range by the tall buildings around although it is a prominent landmark from almost any other part of the city. St Mary's is the mother church of Nottingham. There was certainly a church on the site in Norman times; probably in Saxon times. But what you see today is basically a fifteenth century church; a church in essentially one style; Perpendicular architecture almost at its very best. St Mary's is one of those fine town churches, like St. Peter Mancroft at Norwich and St Mary Redcliffe at Bristol, that reflect the growing prosperity, piety—and perhaps a dash of pomposity—of the medieval merchants. Here, in St Mary's, they worshipped; these Samons, Plumptres, Thurlands, whose monuments you may find among the many interesting ones in the church, thanking God—and the sheep—from whom all blessings flowed. You will find the names of some of these enterprising merchants and Mayors elsewhere in Nottingham; Plumptre Hospital for poor widows has had a Plumptre among its governors or trustees continuously since its foundation in 1390; Thurland Street was opened over the site of the recently demolished Thurland Hall in 1831; but it is in St Mary's that you feel the presence of these dynasties of prosperous townsfolk.

It is not entirely inappropriate that St Mary's is now hemmed in on its eastern and northern side by commercial buildings—and commercial buildings on a vast scale that the tourist usually finds daunting. It would be a pity, however, not to take a closer look at what David Smith in *Industrial Archaeology of the East Midlands* has described as 'a number of fine examples of Victorian commercial architecture at its best'. This area of central Nottingham, once occupied by spacious residences, including, ironically, Plumptre House, was cleared about the middle of the nineteenth century to make way for what is still called the Lace Market.

No historically minded visitor should miss seeing the Lace Market. It is a unique Victorian commercial island in the heart of the city. It is a good idea to walk from the Park, where these lace kings lived, to St Mary's, where they worshipped, and on to the Lace Market, where they made their fortunes. Go, if possible, at the weekend. As David Smith says: 'In the peace of a Saturday afternoon or a Sunday morning, broken only by the sound of the bells of St. Mary's, the imaginative visitor can experience something of the atmosphere of Nottingham at the peak of the lace industry's prosperity.'

The Lace Market was never a market in the sense that lace was sold there to the general public; it was an area in which many lace manufacturers built their offices and warehouses, carried out some of the industrial processes and accepted orders from the trade. The use of the past tense there may be misleading; the Nottingham lace trade is far from dead. Indeed, as F. A. Wells wrote in 1966, 'it would be wrong to think of it as a depressed industry. On its reduced scale it is fairly prosperous. . . .'. Its work force is down now to about 5,000 in the Nottingham area, compared with 20,000 in 1911, but as you walk down Stoney Street there are still a few notices offering work for 'experienced iron pressers', or 'indoor or outdoor lockstitch operators', though there are also offices and warehouses to let, and others which are occupied by interlopers from other trades. Fashions change rapidly; the lace industry may revive, but one is not likely again to experience a wave of confidence such as the one which saw the building of these great red-brick blocks rising to six storeys or more to compensate for lack of space. Many of them have a continuous row of windows on the top floor to give light for mending and finishing.

Architecturally, the most interesting buildings are those constructed for Richard Birkin, occupying most of Broadway, and for Thomas Adams that takes up an enormous block between St Mary's Gate and Stoney Street. Both were built in 1855 in similar styles. The Adams building, occupied by that firm for more than a century, is built in the shape of an 'E', like an Elizabethan mansion. Its main entrance, reached by an imposing flight of steps, leads into an entrance hall which is a riot of classical pillars, handsome arches and frilly ironwork that might be considered slightly ostentatious in a stately home, as indeed might the décor of many of the rooms. Certainly no expense was spared here. There is even a small chapel for the use of the workers. The Birkin building is equally impressive, but makes more use of stone for quoins and doorway and window features.

Another side of the atmosphere of that period can be recaptured by visiting the Theatre Royal in Upper Parliament Street, up the hill to the north of Old Market Square. Designed in 1865 by Phipps, the architect of several London theatres, for the Lambert family, successful dyers, it has enough glitter, glamour and vivacity to gladden the heart of J. B. Priestley and other lovers of the Victorian and Edwardian theatre. A recent modernization has done nothing to spoil its character. I hope that Nottingham people will continue to cherish it as a live theatre—and as a period piece.

Nottingham is indeed fortunate—quite remarkably so in a city with a population, on paper anyway, of only 300,000—in being able to support two professional theatres, and can preen itself in having, in the Playhouse, one of the finest modern theatres in Britain. It began life just after the war with weekly repertory in a small converted cinema. The present theatre, designed by Peter More, opened in 1963. It has a cylindrical auditorium seating 750 with ample leg room and an excellent view of the stage. Under John Neville the productions set a high standard which has been worthily maintained under Peter Burge.

A decade later, it is possible to see the opening of the Playhouse as a major step in a post-war renaissance in Nottingham. The foundation of the Nottingham Festival in 1965 was a second step. Held annually during a fortnight in July, its events have spilled out beyond the city boundaries to places as far distant as Worksop, Retford and Newark, but unfortunately the inevitable financial problems are threatening to restrict its future activities.

Another particularly good time to be in Nottingham is during the three days from the first Thursday in October. At noon on that day the Lord Mayor, with traditional ceremony, declares the opening of the Goose Fair, one of England's oldest, largest and best known fairs. Nobody knows just when it started, but it was an established eight days' fair by 1284. It was held about the time of the Feast of St Matthew (21 September) but the calendar revision of 1752 has thrown it back into October, and the decline of the trading fair has changed its role, and gradually reduced its duration from eight days to three. Although increasing traffic has caused its banishment from the town centre to the large open space called the Forest, it remains as much an integral part of Nottingham life as the Castle itself. Geese may no longer flock along the roads from as far away as Norfolk and Lincolnshire to be sold for traditional Michaelmas fare, but people still flock in from the surrounding countryside to take part in the fun, as they have done for probably a thousand years.

The Forest has its own place in British social history. It was there that a group of young men, mainly Nottinghamshire cricketers keeping themselves fit in the winter, used to kick a ball around. Then in 1861 they formed themselves into a club called Nottingham County Football Club, Britain's oldest League football club. They play now at Meadow Lane, not far from Trent Bridge. Their rivals—Nottingham Forest—the third oldest League club—play on the far side of the river close to Trent Bridge cricket ground. In fact neither of these latter two grounds is in Nottingham at all, but in the urban district of West Bridgford, whose successful fight over the years to retain its independent status can only be attributed to the wealth and influence of many of its inhabitants.

However, as most people think of the Trent Bridge ground as being in Nottingham, it must be mentioned in the Nottingham chapter. It is one of the oldest county grounds in the country, having been laid out in 1838 by William Clarke, a gifted cricketer who had married the landlady of what is now the Trent Bridge Hotel, and who was bringing All England sides to play there long before the County Championship began in 1873. It is rather strange that in these days, when books on both cricket and architecture are numerous, nobody seems to have written a book on what might be called 'cricket pavilion architecture'. When they do, I am sure that Trent Bridge pavilion, a charming building, and its adjoining anachronistic 'Ladies' Pavilion' will feature prominently. Perhaps it is because I saw my first county match there, but Trent Bridge always seems to me to have an elegance, charm and atmosphere that can only be equalled by Lords amongst the bigger cricket grounds.

Trent Bridge itself spans more than a thousand years of history. The first bridge on the site was erected about 922. Until the mid-eighteenth century there was no other bridge over the Trent upstream nearer than Swarkestone in Derbyshire, about 25 miles away. The original bridge was probably of wood, though some of the timber was gradually replaced by stone. There was a major restoration in 1158, and the restored bridge, a mere 12 feet wide, had 17 arches on oak piles. It had on it a chapel in which prayers were offered for travellers and for those who had contributed to the upkeep of the bridge. In 1457 the bridge wardens reported dramatically that 'the bridge fell down for want of repairs', and though repairs were carried out they were insufficient to withstand the great flood of 1683. Its successor, which Defoe called 'a stately stone bridge of 19 arches', was no more trouble-free. Three stone arches had to be replaced by brick ones within 20 years, and there was further flood damage in 1726. By 1849 the bridge was 'narrow, incommodious and in a dangerous state'. The Corporation, discouraged by a £30,000 estimate for a new bridge, sat tight for another 18 years. Then their own surveyor reported the bridge 'inadequate for the traffic over it, insecure in foundations and structure, obstructive to the passage of flood waters and incapable of being satisfactorily altered or repaired'. They took the hint and built a new one, slightly lower down stream, which was opened in 1871. Its width of 40 feet was handsome enough for the horse traffic of those days but quite inadequate for the motor car age. In 1926 its width was doubled, but since then the traffic flow has also more than doubled, as three main roads converge a few yards south of the bridge.

Trent Bridge may be a place to avoid in the rush hour; at other times it is delightful. The Embankment between the bridge and the newly threatened toll-bridge at Wilford is a popular spot on a warm day and there are river trips down to Colwick, the scene of Nottingham's racecourse and its river port. It may be news to many people that Nottingham is an inland port. It is in fact one of the furthest inland in the country, and handles nearly half a million tons of general merchandise a year.

Nottingham people are very attached to what they regard as their river and it is hardly surprising that one of its most successful citizens should have adopted the name for his title. Lord Trent may be better remembered outside the city as Sir Jesse Boot, founder of the local firm that made good with a chain of nationwide chemist shops, but in Nottingham, and in academic circles, he is revered for his gift in 1920 of the magnificent Highfields site, two miles west of the city centre, on which to build a new University College on more spacious surroundings than the old College where Lawrence studied in Shakespeare Street. The new buildings were opened by George V in 1928. University status was achieved in 1948.

The Jesse Boot story followed the traditional rags to riches pattern, but with an unhappy twist at the end as he was for 30 years crippled with rheumatoid arthritis. He began his working life at 13 helping his widowed mother in her herbalist's shop in Hockley. Twenty-five years later, in 1888, Boots Pure Drug Co. was formed and began to manufacture its own drugs in Nottingham. By 1896, the year before Nottingham was granted city status, the firm owned a chain of 60 shops.

In a chapel a few yards from Mrs Boot's shop, William Booth, founder of the Salvation Army, began preaching. He was born in 1829, in even humbler circumstances than Boot, at Sneinton (pronounced Snenton), two miles from the city centre. When the Salvation Army was formed in 1877 he became its first general, and remained in office until his death in 1912.

Australians sometimes find their way out to Sneinton Hollows to see the Bendigo Inn with a statue over the front entrance of William Abednigo Thomson (Bendigo) whose popularity extended to Australia, where the people of Sandhurst in Victoria insisted on changing their city's name to Bendigo. He was born in Parliament Street, Nottingham, in 1811, the twenty-first and youngest child of a mechanic in the lace trade. The last three children were triplet boys, known as Shadrach, Meshach and Abednigo. When Bendigo was 15 his father died, the family had to split up, and he spent some time in a workhouse. Fame came to him suddenly when he took up prize-fighting for a living at the age of 21. In his first year he had eight fights—and won them all. One was against the hitherto unbeaten champion of England, a character called Deaf Burke. They met at Heather in Leicestershire before 12,000 spectators, and Bendigo won in ten rounds to become the new champion.

During his 18 years in the ring he lost only one fight. This was his second contest against a local rival, Ben Caunt of Hucknall Torkard, who at 15 stone was three stone the heavier. In their first meeting, Caunt had been disqualified for striking Bendigo while he sat in his corner after the twenty-second round. The return match went to the seventy-fifth round. Then Bendigo, wearing his ordinary boots for some reason, slipped on the damp turf and fell, whereupon the referee, who had probably had enough even if the pugilists had not, gave the fight to Caunt. But in September 1845, Bendigo had the last blow, though not until the third fight had gone to 93 rounds. At that point, Caunt was so exhausted that he fell without being hit, and the referee declared Bendigo the winner.

Five years later—still reigning champion—Bendigo retired from the ring. Then things went wrong. He did some coaching, but hit too hard to please his pupils. He kept a pub, but was too kind-hearted to refuse drinks his admirers pressed on him, and became an alcoholic. As he was rather given to re-fighting old battles when under the influence, he went to prison 28 times.

But just when he seemed to be down and out, he heard an evangelist preaching, and began his last and hardest fight. Drink was his opponent, and as usual Bendigo won. He devoted the last years of his life to evangelism, and won a local reputation as a preacher. Then, in the summer of 1880, he slipped, as he had done in that second fight with Caunt, but this time on the stairs of his bachelor home at Beeston, and this time there was no return match. Thousands of people crowded to see his funeral in St Mary's Cemetery, in Bath Street, Nottingham, now a Garden of Rest. Later they erected a monument there, the life-sized figure of a recumbent lion.

Bendigo seems to me to typify one aspect of Nottingham, the slightly raffish, virile, determined Nottingham that emerges in *Saturday Night and Sunday Morning* by the locally born Alan Sillitoe. It is a long way from the Nottingham of Marshal Tallard, and yet that facet of the city's character has also survived even though its appearance is changing with the banishment of the motor car from the centre and the conversion of one of its main railway stations into the vast Victoria shopping centre. It is not easy to sum up the essential character of Nottingham. It is not 'that dismal town' of D. H. Lawrence, nor does it grow 'beastlier and beastlier', as Hilaire Belloc thought, any more than it is the 'Paradise restored' that Thomas Baskerville thought he saw in the seventeenth century. Let us leave the last words to A. L. Rowse, who said it was a place from which one took away 'A very real sense of inspiration, an impression of marked public spirit, a feeling of pride in the past, of confidence in the future' and who called Nottingham 'a magnificent town, full of improbable splendours'.

CHAPTER THREE

The Erewash Valley

Lawrence Country

You can miss the Erewash Valley if you wish. Many tourists do, unless they are ardent D. H. Lawrence enthusiasts. Like Mr Squeers, its appearance is not immediately prepossessing. A hurried drive along the Valley on any of the various main roads that run north-westwards from Nottingham is apt to leave an impression of drab little Victorian towns struggling rather desperately and belatedly to adopt most of the worst features of modern urban life; of slag heaps and collieries, some of them abandoned and desolate; of fading terraced houses and modern 'semis' that look a little brighter because they are newer rather than through any intrinsic attractiveness.

That may be one's first impression. It is, I believe, a false one. I must immediately declare an interest here, being born in the Valley—admittedly a mile on the Derbyshire side—and it is difficult to be objective about an area where one's roots lie. But I am with Bridget Pugh whose pamphlet,[1] *The Country of My Heart*, is an indispensable guide to the Lawrence country, in saying that 'the country-side is unexpectedly beautiful'.

Perhaps the beauty lies in the unexpectedness. You hardly expect to find beauty in a mining country and often the average traveller only sees what he expects to see. To find the loveliness that has not been quite ruined in the Valley you have to look beyond the head-stocks, between the slag heaps, or from the back gardens of those drab terraces. It is a beauty on a small scale, and if it is not the sort of beauty that tourists drive miles to see, it is none the worse for that. Often it is mixed up with much that is unsightly; if one bend in the road shows you some of the worst kinds of dereliction that the Industrial Revolution fathered on the English countryside, the next bend may offer

[1]Nottinghamshire Local History Council, 1972.

something as lovely as you can find anywhere in the East Midlands.

Such beauty owes little to the river itself. Most rivers have some attractive features; the Erewash has very few. It is a narrow, undistinguished stream, hardly noticeable except when it bursts its banks. It rises just south of Kirkby-in-Ashfield and wriggles a serpentine way for some 20 miles before joining the Trent in a place of empty country nearly opposite Barton-in-Fabis about eight miles south-west of Nottingham. For some of its course it keeps close company with the Erewash Canal, once an important waterway, but now kept open by the efforts of local boating enthusiasts, and for even more, it forms the boundary with Derbyshire. The valley, in a strictly geographical sense, is often less than a mile wide and uncommonly steep-sided in places, but even when defined loosely in Lawrence's sense to include the homogeneous surrounds, it is not much more than five miles wide, screened on the western horizon by the hills at the southern end of the Derbyshire Peak, and eastward, much closer, by tree-lined slopes that are the outliers of the old Sherwood Forest.

The landscape of the valley is an old industrial scene superimposed on a still older agricultural one; a palimpsest on which the earlier writing still shows, so that you may find haystacks behind the headstocks and cattle grazing under the lee of a factory wall. When I was a boy, many a miner cultivated a small-holding with what energy he could muster after a long day in the pit, and this breed has not entirely vanished. Spiritually, as well as geographically, the Erewash Valley miner is still very close to the countryside. His hobbies are likely to be out-door affairs. Whippet racing may not be as popular as it was in the 1930s, but every row of miners' houses is likely to have its pigeon lofts and at least some lovingly tended gardens. It is not long ago since Lawrence's father, on his way to work at Brinsley pit, 'would set off in the dawn across the fields at Coney Grey, and hunt for mushrooms in the long grass, or perhaps pick up a skulking rabbit, which he would bring home at evening inside the lining of his pit coat'. This sort of tradition has lingered on. When I was a boy, life in the valley was still what Lawrence called 'a curious cross between industrialism and the old agricultural England of Shakespeare and Milton and Fielding and George Eliot', and I suspect that it is still.

Of course, the industrial tradition goes back a long way too. Queen Eleanor, wife of Henry III, hurriedly moved from Nottingham Castle to Tutbury in 1257 because the air in the town was so polluted by 'sea-coal'. This coal almost certainly came from the Erewash Valley, where the seams came to the surface. The monks of Beauvale Priory outcropped coal at Selston in the thirteenth century, and a lease issued to seven men of Cossall in 1316 indicates that the workings there were of some depth, for the rent could be remitted if work stopped through flooding or 'le damp', the earliest reference anywhere in England to the choke-damp that could be lethal in ill-ventilated pits. As the lease also refers to a gutter, or sough, by which water would be drained from the workings it is clear that bell-pits (bell-shaped mines) had already been introduced. Most of this coal was probably used locally for lime-burning, brewing, baking and iron-smelting, but by the early sixteenth century a flourishing pit at Wollaton, close to Nottingham and the Trent, developed markets much farther afield. And from 1580 to 1588 the packhorses that carried coal to Ancaster in Lincolnshire brought back stone for the building of Wollaton Hall.

Historically, then, Wollaton is the best place to start a tour of the Erewash Valley, though geographically it is not ideal for it will involve some to-ing and fro-ing over the same ground, and in truth the Hall and Park belong to Nottingham, whose Corporation bought the estate, now lying within the city's extended boundary, for £200,000 in 1925. The entrance for motorists is just off the Ilkeston road (A 609), two miles west of the city centre, and the park extends to the valley's edge.

Wollaton Hall is an important house nationally because it was one of the first great mansions to be built mainly out of industrial profits. Its builder, Sir Francis Willoughby, was more than a coal-owner; his interests included an iron works, the manufacture of glass and the growing of woad for dyers. His family had already been prominent in Nottinghamshire for more than three centuries, though during that time there had been a change of surname. The founder of the family fortunes was a Nottingham merchant named Ralph Bugge, who around 1240, bought an estate at Willoughby-on-the-Wolds. His grandson, on being knighted, called himself 'Sir Richard de Willoughby', presumably because it seemed more suited to the manner of life to which he hoped to become accustomed. The Wollaton estates came into the family through the marriage of his son, also Sir Richard, to the heiress of the de Morteins of Wollaton, whose manor

house was near the church, but it appears that they did not immediately move, as the earliest Willoughby monument in the church
dates from 1471.

Another monument there is to 'Mr Robert Smythson, gent,
architector and surveyor unto the most worthy house of Wollaton',
who died in 1614, but there is, surprisingly, not one to Sir Francis, who
spent more than £8,000—a pretty considerable sum then—to build
the mansion. The expense of building and maintaining the 'prodigy
house', entertaining lavishly, keeping up a household of '46 persones',
and paying heavy dowries for three daughters left him deeply in debt.
He quarrelled with his family and died unhappily alone in London.

But the Hall itself is sufficient memorial, though to reinforce the
memory there is a Latin couplet engraved on the south front:

> *En has Francisi Willughbi militis aedes*
> *Rara arte extructas Willughbaeisq [ue] relictas.*
> *Inchoatae 1580 et finitae 1588.*
> *Behold this house of Francis Willoughby, knight,*
> *With rare art built, to Willoughbys bequeathed.*
> *Begun 1580 and finished 1588.*

Rare art, indeed! But then, Robert Smythson was an artist in
stone, and, incidentally, one of the earliest of his profession to be
described as an architect. He had already worked at Longleat as
master mason and was shortly to build Hardwick Hall in neighbouring
Derbyshire. Hardwick is flamboyant enough, but more restrained
than Wollaton, where Willoughby, clearly eager to keep ahead of the
Joneses, left no stone undecorated. The result is a sort of fairy-tale
palace; a rich confection of towers, pavilions, balustrades, pinnacles
and statues, adorning a perfect hill-top site. It is in sober fact a square
house of two storeys, with its corner pavilions adding a third storey
and its central tower above the great hall rising higher still. Some architectural purists dislike it, and Pevsner shrewdly sees a kinship 'with
some Victorian imitation Tudor *châteaux*', but my first view of it
early on a summer's morning when only the towers were visible
above the mist remains vividly in my mind. I fell in love with it then,
and though I can now see its imperfections—nearly 200 statues are a
bit much—my affection is steadfast.

Admittedly, the interior is rather disappointing, apart from the great hall and the ceilings above the two staircases. The hall, rising 50 feet to its hammer-beam roof, was designed to impress, and succeeds. The paintings on the ceilings used to be attributed to Verrio or Laguerre, but recent research has established that Sir James Thornhill, Hogarth's father-in-law, was responsible with Laguerre for most of the work. The rest of the rooms that most visitors see—conducted tours of the remainder can be arranged—have been adapted to house Nottingham Corporation's natural history museum. That the house should be used for this purpose might have saddened its builder, but it would doubtless have delighted Francis Willoughby (1635–72), the famous naturalist and friend of John Ray, who fathered both the first Willoughby Baronet and the first Baron Middleton. Of the rest of the family, the best known was Sir Hugh Willoughby, the explorer, who, along with some 70 members of his two ships' companies, was found frozen to death in the Arctic in 1555 when he was trying to find a north-east passage to Cathay and India. A second museum is housed in the courtyard of the stable block. This is an industrial museum containing machinery from the hosiery, textile, tobacco, bicycle and other industries that have assisted in making Nottingham's fortune. It is in its infancy and at the time of writing, opens only on Thursdays, Saturdays and on Sunday afternoons, but as it grows it will probably be open more often. The stables themselves, with an imposing Georgian Classical façade, are large enough and handsome enough, to be a stately home.

Wollaton Park, in which deer still roam, is enclosed by a wall which local tradition asserts to be seven miles long and to have taken seven men with seven apprentices seven years to build. The enclosure probably led to the destruction of Sutton Passeys village, last mentioned in a subsidy roll of 1558 and now remembered only by a nearby Sutton Passeys Crescent. The Park originally covered 802 acres, but when Nottingham Corporation bought the estate from Lord Middleton they sold 274 acres for building development, which explains why a splendid Tudor gatehouse stands unexpectedly anchored in a sea of houses alongside the Derby Road. The sale more than covered the purchase cost and still left sufficient parkland to accommodate the Royal Show of 1955. In fact the showground, then the largest ever provided for the Royal in its peripatetic days, covered only one fifth of the park.

Wollaton village, by-passed in the 1930s, remains what eighteenth-century topographers would have described enthusiastically as a 'neat village'. It is a surprisingly peaceful backwater to find so near to the city and its centre by the church is quiet and leafy. The parish church, dedicated to St Leonard, a French nobleman, has the battlemented tower and short spire typical of this part of the county. It is basically a fourteenth-century church with nineteenth-century additions, and, according to a tablet in the nave, was 'restored and beautified through the generosity of many 1968–71'. These latest alterations, made necessary not only by deteriorating stonework but also by the need to find additional seating for worshippers in a parish whose population has increased from 700 to 24,000 in 50 years, have also involved the moving of the altar from the east wall to a more central position west of the choir stalls in the prevailing liturgical fashion. The woodwork of the rare and splendid seventeenth-century Classical reredos with its fluted Corinthian columns has been covered with white emulsion paint, which may not please everyone but certainly adds light to the building, as does the very attractive modern glass in the porch. The monuments, mostly to Willoughbys, are numerous and good. A pleasantly ill-spaced and ill-spelt tablet over a nave arch proclaims that:

> *Near unto this place lyeth interred the body*
> *of Thomas Man, Dr. of Phys-*
> *sick and Fellow of Jesus*
> *Colledge in Cambridge*
> *who died Anno Dom*
> 1690

A medieval cottage nearly opposite the church is thought to have been connected with the old manor house, traces of which have been found fairly recently under the former rectory. The other houses around are mainly early eighteenth century, mostly brick though there is some stonework. The Admiral Rodney has been modernised, but is still an attractive white-fronted inn and the buildings behind are obviously eighteenth century.

A right turn at the traffic lights on the Ilkeston road at the western edge of Wollaton takes you along the B6004, which neatly separates the vast Bilborough housing estate on the right, from the green belt on

53

the left. The first left turn leads to Strelley, where the lane peters out at the far end of the park wall of Strelley Hall. Strelley is an even more remarkable survival than Wollaton, for while Wollaton has managed to retain the illusion of a quiet village in the midst of suburbia, Strelley is a genuine country village less than five miles from Nottingham's Slab Square. The reason for this happy survival—apart from the wisdom of modern planners, and contrary to general opinion, modern planners quite often are wise—appear to be threefold: that its village street leads nowhere, that it has always been a squirarchal village, and that it got over its industrial revolution early enough to allow for recovery. That Strelley should ever have been an industrial village, may now seem impossible. But traces of the old bell pits are still visible to sharp-eyed industrial archaeologists. At the beginning of the seventeenth century, these pits were producing 20,000 tons of coal a year, half the total for the whole country. They were owned by Percival Willoughby of Wollaton, but leased by Huntingdon Beaumont, a member of a Leicestershire family with literary as well as industrial leanings. It was Beaumont, apparently, who conceived the idea of laying a wooden waggonway two miles in length from the pits southward to Wollaton Lane, the main road to Nottingham. This prototype line, probably laid between October 1603 and October 1604, was the earliest ancestor of the railways. Traces of an old waggonway track can still be seen near the old bell pits in fields west of the B6004 about 200 yards south of the road to Strelley.

As for the squires of Strelley, there were two families; the Strelleys and the Edges. The Strelleys remained in unbroken succession from Norman times to 1678 when Ralph Edge, thrice Mayor of Nottingham, bought the estate. His descendants are still there, in a rather gaunt Georgian house that is not open to the public but can be seen quite well from the churchyard. The gardens are sometimes open in summer. For the Strelleys you have to look in the complete fourteenth-century church, 'without any doubt the most important church on the western outskirts of Nottingham', according to Pevsner. Their tombs are in the superb chancel, which is separated from the nave by 'the finest rood screen in Nottinghamshire'. The best monument is to Sir Sampson de Strelley, who built the church around 1356. It takes the form of a tomb-chest of Derbyshire alabaster, on which his

10. (opposite, above) *Mattersey Church, from the south*

11. (below) *Teversal Church looking east, showing seventeenth-century box pews and squire's pew*

armoured effigy lies holding his wife's hand; his feet rest on a lion, hers on two puppies. The carving was probably done in Nottingham.

From Strelley, it is best to retrace one's steps to the traffic lights and then go straight ahead for Stapleford. On the way is Moor Farm, now a sophisticated restaurant, but still bearing traces of its mediaeval origins, and the Hemlock Stone, an isolated pillar of Bunter sandstone rising 30 feet above a green hillock like an overgrown toadstool. There are, of course, many legends about the Hemlock Stone, some concerned with Druids, and another, repeated about other stones in various parts of Britain with slight variations, that it was thrown by the Devil at an Abbot of Lenton, but fell short by a few miles. The truth is that it is the surviving portion of a cliff of soft sandstone of which the rest has long since eroded away. The Hemlock Stone survived because its sand grains are naturally cemented together by barium sulphate. Lawrence rather unkindly described it as 'a little, gnarled, twisted stump of rock, something like a decayed mushroom, standing out pathetically on the side of a field'. Many people find it quite impressive, and the tangled undergrowth above it is a favourite picnic spot, from which there are wide but largely urban views.

Stapleford, when you drive along its main street, strikes you as being as dull a little town as you will find anywhere in England, being seemingly Victorian in origin and now devoting its life to the manufacture of hosiery, pencils, furniture and other aids to gracious living. But very few English towns are completely without their saving graces and Stapleford is no exception. It has in its main street, the old Derby-Nottingham road, a row of stockingers' cottages, probably dating from the early nineteenth century, with the long row of windows on the top floor—as in some of the lace buildings mentioned in Chapter Two—to give more light to the homeworkers at their framework knitting machines. More importantly, it has in its churchyard the finest Saxon cross in the county. This was not its original site, which was just outside the churchyard, and the top and base were renewed in 1820, but the shaft, ten feet high and carved with interlacings and one human figure must be at least 1,000 years old. The churchyard gates are a pleasant example of early Victorian ironwork and the church itself is another interesting example of mainly fourteenth century architecture with the usual local battlemented tower and short spire, a good east window and an unusual domed iron font

12. (opposite, above) *Thoresby Hall. The Great Hall*

13. (below) *Welbeck Abbey, seat of the Dukes of Portland, but now mainly occupied by an army preparatory college*

cover of about 1660. There is also a rather ugly monument to Admiral Sir John Borlase Warren (1753–1822), and his son George, who was killed in action after landing at Aboukir in Egypt in 1801.

The Admiral was a local boy who made good when his boyhood was well behind him. His birthplace, Stapleford Hall, has long since gone, but several pubs in the district perpetuate his name. Destined by his parents for the Church, he twice ran away to sea from Cambridge, before unexpectedly inheriting the family estates and a revived baronetcy when his three elder brothers died in rapid succession. His newly acquired wealth enabled him to buy Lundy Island and a commission in the Navy, as well as to pay the debts of all naval officers then in debtors' prisons. But he was over 40 when he won fame at sea. His greatest triumph was in thwarting a French invasion of Ireland in 1798 by a crushing victory over the supporting squadron. He was M.P. for Nottingham from 1796 to 1806 and later became Ambassador to Russia, then—at 68—Commander-in-Chief of the North American station.

The road southward from Stapleford church—labelled B6003—runs parallel with the Erewash at about a mile's distance, has nothing much to offer apart from a distant view ahead of the Charnwood Forest in Leicestershire and some splendid rose gardens. In fact, the whole area on both sides of the Trent from Stapleford to Edwalton, south-east of Nottingham, is one of the best for rose growing in the country. In a fairly heavily built-up area less than 500 acres of land produces over five million rose bushes a year to the value of about £1 million. The reason for the success of this rose-growing industry that sprang up about 1860 seems to lie in the quality of the Keuper Marl, that retains moisture in a comparatively dry area without becoming too stiff, and, of course, in the green fingers of the producers.

There are rose gardens along the A52 almost into Nottingham, but this is rather too far outside the Erewash Valley. A right turn round the island where the old Derby road meets the new one takes you into Bramcote, another village that has managed to retain some character despite its proximity to Nottingham. It too has an interesting row of stockingers' cottages on the main road, just east of the road junction, but most of the village straggles pleasantly up the hillside just off the B6003, which cuts through the rock quite impressively at the summit. On the right-hand side is the fourteenth-century tower of the old church, all that was left standing when a new one was built lower down the hill in 1861. The old tower is known locally as the 'Sunken Church', and at first glance it does look as if it is gradually sinking into the earth, but this is an illusion, possibly caused in part by the surrounding ground having been built up by rubble from the demolished fabric of the rest of the building. Opposite the tower is a pleasing late Georgian house with a central Venetian window. A few yards away on the corner of Cow Lane, at this point as rural as its name, stand a pair of nineteenth-century almshouses, erected by Frances Jane Longdon. Just to the south, where the road descends towards Chilwell, is the Manor House, basically a Jacobean or earlier house with steep gables and mullioned windows, 'one of the best brick buildings in Nottinghamshire', in Pevsner's judgment.

Chilwell, like its neighbour Toton, is largely subtopian, though in both villages there are still houses that survive from an agricultural past. Chilwell has a large ordnance depot, the scene of a disastrous explosion in 1918 that killed 141 people and was distinctly heard by my parents in their garden 15 miles away. It also had a haunted cottage in which there were strange goings on more than a century ago. Things went bump in the night so frequently that eventually nobody would live in the house and it had to be demolished. But its reputation survived. The site, now on a council estate but still known as 'Ghost House Lane', has been deliberately left vacant. Toton has one of the largest railway marshalling yards in Europe, handling over 4,000 wagons, mostly coal wagons, a day, but the yards are inaccessible to train spotters.

In fact there are more trains to be spotted from the level-crossing gates at Attenborough station, the first of a series of crossings that separate various main roads from the north bank of the Trent to the outskirts of Newark on the branch line from Derby to Lincoln. The crossing gates at Attenborough appear to form something of a social barrier. To live south of the tracks here is manifestly a sign that one has arrived. In fact Attenborough may well be up at arms in being discussed in an Erewash Valley chapter; the village belongs unmistakably to the Trent Valley. Yet its inclusion here can be justified because the Erewash joins the Trent a mere mile from Attenborough church. Attenborough is one of those villages where the young girls walk around in jodhpurs and the summer silence is disturbed only by by the sounds of lawn mowers—motor mowers—behind tall hedges. Even the church is hidden discreetly behind hedges and tall trees, though its spire, rising from the usual battlemented tower, is a conspicuous landmark from both railway and river. It is in fact a rather larger spire than most of its neighbours and the church itself is surprisingly large. The nave dates from about 1269, and the arches and pillars that divide it from aisles that were added perhaps a century later are good examples of late Norman work, the arches being pointed with dog-toothed moulding. Two good poppyhead pew ends from the twelfth century now stand at the entrance to the chancel door. Incorporated in the modern choir stalls are fragments of Jacobean carvings with mermen and mermaids, depicting the arms of the Powtrill and Ireton families. The Powtrills must have been particularly proud of their arms, which appear in at least two other places in the church, but it is the Iretons who are better remembered, especially Henry, and to a lesser extent his brother John.

They were born in the house that adjoins the churchyard and baptised in the present thirteenth-century font, Henry on 3 November 1611, and his brother four years later. Henry went to Trinity College, Oxford, and studied law at Middle Temple, but it is as a soldier that he is remembered. He fought as a cavalry captain at Edgehill under the Earl of Essex, received a thigh wound and was taken prisoner at Naseby but soon escaped to become one of Cromwell's Major-Generals, as well as the husband of Cromwell's daughter Bridget, whom he married in 1646. He was an articulate man; 'the best prayer-maker and preacher' in an army that was not deficient in these qualities. Even Cromwell found him a bit wordy: 'I write not to thy husband', he wrote to Bridget, 'partly to avoid trouble, for one line of mine begets many of his . . .' and we recall that he was nicknamed 'the Scribe'. But Ireton was an able and honest man who refused to accept £2,000 out of the confiscated estates of the Duke of Buckingham. He tried hard to save the king until he found that Charles was not to be trusted. 'He gave me words', said Ireton, 'and we paid him in his own coin, when we found he had no real intention for the people's good, but to prevail by our factions and to regain by art what he had lost in fight.' He was a member of the court that condemned the king. Afterwards he went to Ireland and had just succeeded Cromwell as Lord Deputy when he caught the plague and died at Limerick in

1651. His body was brought back to London, laid in state at Somerset House and was buried in the Henry VII chapel in Westminster Abbey. Later his remains were dug up, carried to Tyburn on a hurdle, hanged on a gibbet and buried at its foot at sunset. His brother John, who had been Lord Mayor of London, was imprisoned and then transported to the Scilly Isles.

The extensive gravel workings between Attenborough village and the Trent have yielded evidence of occupation in the Bronze Age. These gravel pits are no longer worked and now form a most attractive nature reserve, open to the public. From the Trent bank, over the reserve, one gets a most felicitous picture of Attenborough, a charming, leafy village.

Beeston, its eastern neighbour, was another gravel terrace village, but it has long since sprawled over from its terrace to become a sizeable town. It is not just a dormitory of Nottingham, which it adjoins, but an industrial town in its own right whose daytime population is greater than its residential population. It has made the gradual transition common to the area from an agricultural village to a framework knitting centre and on to lace-making until it has become a general industrial centre. Though not the sort of place to which tourists usually flock, it has considerable attractions for industrial archaeologists. One of its most interesting buildings historically is the surviving portion of the Humber works at the junction of Queen's Road and Humber Road. It is a reminder of the importance of the Nottingham district in the early bicycle industry. Workers trained to handle small metal parts for hosiery and lace-machine making easily adapted themselves to the very similar skills required in the cycle trade.

The first Nottingham bicycles appeared in the 1860s and by the end of the century there were some 60 firms in the industry. Thomas Humber, who had already some experience with William Campion, the first Nottingham cycle-maker, began to make his own machines in a workshop that still stands in Stretton Street, Nottingham. Outgrowing this and a second larger factory, he moved out to Beeston in 1880 and was employing well over 1,000 workers by the end of the century, some of whom lived in company houses that still adjoin the works. When, like other bicycle manufacturers, including the future Lord Nuffield, he started producing motor cars as a sideline, there was need for still more space. In 1908 the firm abandoned the Beeston factory to the lace trade and moved to Coventry, where it already had a branch factory suitable for extension.

One of the oldest surviving lace factories in the district, dating probably from the reign of William IV, when the trade was extending westwards from Nottingham, is situated in Villa Street. It was owned in the 1860s by William Felkin Junior, son of the historian of the lace and hosiery trades. He told a Parliamentary committee in 1861 that the factory employed two sets of operatives, women, young persons and children, who kept the machines going for 20 hours a day. The first shift worked from 4 a.m. to 9 a.m. and 1 p.m. to 6 p.m. The second worked the intervening periods, finishing at midnight, except on Saturdays when work stopped for the weekend at 5 p.m.

Apart from a shallow hipped roof, this four-storey factory is severely functional, like most nineteenth-century industrial buildings in the area, but a notable exception is the Anglo-Scotian Mills on Wollaton Road. The unknown architect of this building, erected in the 1870s to manufacture lace curtains and Shetland knitwear, fairly let himself go with hexagonal crenellated turrets on either side of the pointed Gothic main entrance and on the corners of the façade, Gothic windows and crenellations above patterned brickwork running along the entire length of the main front. The word *LABORAMUS* on two pseudo-heraldic shields above the main entrance were probably intended as a warning that frivolity was confined to the exterior of the building.

We have strayed slightly out of the Erewash Valley at Beeston, but it is a short run back to the traffic lights on Ilkeston Road at Balloon Houses on the western edge of Wollaton. From there it is a pleasant ride of two miles through a green belt to Trowell, which has an imposing fifteenth-century church tower, two or three good old farmhouses, an impressive industrial landscape of British Steel Corporation's Stanton Ironworks on the Derbyshire side of the Erewash—for those who are prepared to be impressed by that sort of view—a quantity of modern housing, and a perpetual state of bewilderment that it was chosen as the typical English village for the 1951 Festival of Britain. As the Ilkeston road continues into Derbyshire, we should turn right short of Trowell church, for Cossall, which is much nearer to the usual romanticised picture of a typical English village. Like Strelley, it has had time to recover from its taste of the industrial revolution, though the Nottingham Canal, that keeps the road company for half a mile or so south of the village, still carried boats loaded with coal well within living memory. When I last travelled this road the canal was deserted, except for two young men angling alongside a board which said 'Fishing strictly forbidden', but it was still in good order. There is not much of Cossall, but what there is is quite charming. Old cottages and farmhouses snuggle within the angles formed by two sharp bends in the road. There are traces of a moat behind what Lawrence called 'the old, little church with its small spire on a square tower', and beside the church are the red brick, steep gabled Willoughby almshouses of 1685, 'a delicious group', in Pevsner's words, which nobody could dispute. Cossall is Cossethay in *The Rainbow*. William Brangwen in the book was based on Alfred Burrows, who lived with his family at Church Cottage and carved the reredos in the church. His daughter, Louise, to whom Lawrence was engaged for a time, was Ursula Brangwen. Marsh Farm, where 'the Brangwens had lived for generations', no longer stands 'in the meadows where the Erewash twisted sluggishly through alder trees, separating Derbyshire from Nottinghamshire'. It has been replaced by a modern bungalow.

Beyond Cossall Marsh a single signpost points eastward from the rather dreary, ribbon-built Kimberley road to Babbington. It is worth following this rutty, dispirited lane which peters out into a track just short of its intended destination. Babbington is a most peculiar place. It is no more than a row of cottages, a farm and a larger house built on a shelf on a grassy hillside. The remains of the colliery it was built to serve now lie hidden under grass and scrub. One would expect the hamlet to have died with it, but in fact most of the miners' cottages have been modernised and Babbington has become a surprisingly pleasing small rural dormitory for Nottingham and Ilkeston, which lies on the Derbyshire side of the Erewash.

Behind Babbington the land rises to 450 feet, which is high for these parts and unexpectedly empty apart from scattered farms with attractive names like Turkey Farm, Strelley Park Farm and Chilwell Dam Farm. Up there one can understand Lawrence's reference to the 'extremely beautiful countryside' of his native valley. Back on the main road, however, it is mainly an industrial landscape.

Kimberley is one of those overgrown, switchback villages that are common in west Nottinghamshire. Its most distinctive feature is a working brewery, a rare sight these days in an English village. This one lacks the charm of the honey-coloured Donnington brewery in the Cotswolds. It is a severely functional building, but its position on an outcropping rock above the village gives it, from a distance, some resemblance to an aircraft carrier surrounded by smaller vessels.

Kimberley lies on the main road between Nottingham and Eastwood, and it was on this road in 1817 (long before it acquired its present label of A610) that the Pentrich Revolt fizzled out. It had been a crack-brained scheme from the beginning. A hundred or so disgruntled men from east Derbyshire villages round Pentrich and South Wingfield set out to march on Nottingham, driven to desperation by the appalling conditions then existing in the country under the abrasive government of Lord Liverpool. They were further inflamed by the oratory of a young man from Sutton-in-Ashfield named Jeremiah Brandreth—the self-styled 'Nottingham Captain'—who was probably himself the dupe of a government *agent provocateur*, the notorious Oliver. There, they were persuaded, strong reinforcements would join them in advance on London and the overthrow of the government. On their way they called at various houses to demand arms and recruits, and at one that was barred to them Brandreth senselessly shot and killed a man-servant. This needless killing lowered morale, and some men, further discouraged by reports that soldiers were looking for them, had deserted before the raggle-taggle army crossed the Erewash into Nottinghamshire. The rest reached Giltbrook, about a mile north-west of Kimberley, and were being formed into line when a troop of the 15th Hussars from Nottingham Barracks rode over the brow of the hill and charged. The Pentrich rebels immediately called it a day. They threw down their arms and took to the fields. Brandreth and nearly 50 of his men failed to escape. They were tried at Derby Assizes. Brandreth and two others were executed; 20 more transported; the rest received free pardons.

Along this same road from 1913, the green, cream and gold trams of the Nottinghamshire and Derbyshire Tramway Company on the Nottingham-Ripley service, ran at 15 minute intervals during peak periods. Not that the service actually ran from Nottingham until a year later; in its early days it left from Cinderhill, then just outside the city. And it never quite reached the centre of Ripley; stopping abruptly in the middle of the road outside the Butterley cricket ground on the outskirts, as though suddenly conscious that it was getting out of its depth. Originally, this was planned, during the period of 'tramway mania' around 1903, as just one line in a 79-mile network of tramways covering the whole valley and beyond. For various reasons, including opposition from the Midland Railway, this 14-mile stretch became the only one laid down. Even so, it was reputedly the longest privately owned tramway system in Britain, and indisputably the least comfortable. As a child, I had an ambition to undertake that journey from Nottingham to Ripley by tram, and I can still remember every bump and jolt of its eventual fulfilment. Lawrence, needless to say, captured brilliantly the rhythm of the ride in one of his best essays.

To reach Eastwood by public transport today you must go by bus. Trains no longer stop there. This is ironical, for it was there, in 1832, that the Midland Railway was born, according to a plaque on the wall of the Sun Inn in the Market Place. It might be more accurate to call the Sun the place where the railway was conceived, rather than the actual birthplace; the gestation period was protracted and the infant not quite what its parents hoped for at first, though it eventually grew into a healthy adult.

To be more specific, the railway came into existence because of the fierce competition between the coal-owners of north Leicestershire and the Erewash Valley for the profitable market in and around Leicester. The opening of the Erewash and Cromford and the Lough-borough Navigation in the second half of the eighteenth century had given direct access to Leicester from the pits of Derbyshire and Nottinghamshire. All these canal schemes were strongly opposed by the owners of collieries in north Leicestershire, who had previously sent coal to Leicester by the slow and costly pack-horse and wagon· When the opposition was unsuccessful, the Leicestershire owners built their own Charnwood Forest Canal, but this was an engineering failure. It burst its banks in 1799, was never repaired and soon became derelict, leaving the Nottinghamshire and Derbyshire owners in undisputed possession of the Leicester market. It was to end this monopoly, that rocketed Erewash canal shares from their original £125 to £1,500 each in 1825, that the north Leicestershire men secured an Act for building the Leicester and Swannington Railway in 1830.

The opening of this, the first locomotive hauled railway in the East Midlands, in July 1832, ended a blissful period of over 30 years during which the Erewash Valley collieries had been selling about 160,000 tons of coal a year around Leicester. In an attempt to fight their way back into that market, the Erewash Valley owners called the meeting at the Sun Inn in the following month. Their intention was to open a railway, to be called the Midland Counties Railway, from Pinxton to Leicester. From that small beginning sprang a much bigger project to link Derby and Nottingham, and to connect both towns with London by way of the London and Birmingham Railway. Ironically, when the line was finally sanctioned in 1836, the original Pinxton-Leicester project had been dropped and did not reappear until several years later. The Midland Railway emerged in 1844 as a result of the amalgamation of the Midland Counties, the North Midland and Derby and Birmingham Junction railways, which two years later absorbed the Leicester and Swannington. New lines sprang up in all directions and the Erewash Valley coal-owners eventually won back at least some of the Leicester market.

If Eastwood should be something of a place of pilgrimage for railway historians, it certainly should be so for D. H. Lawrence enthusiasts, and could be much more if the local authority showed a little more enthusiasm for its most famous citizen. The fact is that Eastwood has a curiously ambivalent attitude towards Lawrence. The official guide book of the Eastwood Urban District Council dismisses him in a single oddly guarded sentence: 'During the present century the parish has had the distinction of being chosen as the home of the late D. H. Lawrence, the famous writer, whose books have caused such world-wide controversy, both among the general public and among the critics.' He did not *choose* Eastwood as his home; his parents were living there when he was born and lived there till they died. But there is no mention of his birthplace; no mention of the other four houses in which he lived during the first half—or slightly more—of his life, though there is, it is true, a plaque outside the terraced house in Victoria Street in which he was born in 1875.

The official attitude towards Lawrence seems to reflect the general attitude towards him in the town, at least among the survivors of his own generation; the younger generation are more enthusiastic. Adult education classes on Lawrence and his work tend to fill the schools in other parts of the valley, but in the past anyway, Eastwood has been stonily indifferent. It is difficult to put one's finger on the cause of the trouble. Probably there are several. There may be traces of inverted snobbery, rebelling against the snobbery of Mrs Lawrence, a miner's wife who thought her son too good for the pit, and a feeling that he thought himself too good; or at least, different. That perhaps was the main bone of contention. Despite its strong Nonconformist tradition in religion and politics, an Erewash Valley mining community is intensely conservative socially. Any departure from the norm arouses suspicion. This particularly applies to work. Work is a physical thing. Any man who works with his brain is suspect, though there is a qualified acceptance of certain professional and clerical workers who are clever enough to avoid real hard graft. But artists of any kind do not fall into this category. Theirs is not work at all; they are parasites, and effeminate too. That was the thinking 40 years ago. It may have changed a good deal since then, but not, I fancy, amongst the older people. One reporter who went in search of material about Lawrence some years ago was told: 'He were nowt but a big soft gel.' He was not interested in games and was happier in his Eastwood days with girls than with boys of his own age. There may also be the feeling that Lawrence was disloyal to Eastwood. 'I have always hated it,' he wrote in 1918. That has been remembered. The next sentence of the briefly returned exile, 'Now I don't', has been forgotten by people who recall his disgust at 'the ugliness of my native village', which he wanted pulling down 'to the last brick'.

Perhaps the 'village' has rankled more than the 'ugliness'. Eastwood is unmistakably a town. Equally unmistakably, it is ugly. It is doubtful if it could ever have been made, despite its hill-top position, 'like the lovely hill-towns of Italy, shapely and fascinating', as Lawrence thought it could, though it could certainly have been made a great deal more attractive than it is if the original coal-owners, Barber Walker and Company, and the speculators who followed them, had been less concerned with quick profits. And yet, if you stand outside the birthplace in Victoria Street and look downhill you can see why Lawrence called this 'the county of my heart'. Better still, go to Walker Street, where he lived from 1881 to 1902. 'Go to Walker Street and stand in front of the third house—and look across at Crich on the left, Underwood in front—High Park woods and Annesley on the right: I lived in that house from the age of 6 to 18, and I know that view better than any in the world.' You can still see that view just as Lawrence saw it and understand why he loved the English countryside and hated what man had done to make so much of it so much less lovely.

'Then walk down the fields to the Breach, and in the corner house facing the stile I lived from 1 to 6.' This was the home of the Morels in *Sons and Lovers*. Odd things have happened recently to this house in Garden Road, formerly The Breach. It was bought in 1969, to save it from demolition, by the Association of Young Writers. But as young writers are not usually blessed with full pockets they found it difficult to maintain. Vandals did much damage; there was a fire. The Urban District Council felt disinclined to help over restoration, or to get the house listed for preservation. Demolition seemed to be the only course left. Now the position has changed quite dramatically. The house has been listed by the Department of the Environment and will rank for an improvement grant. Restoration is in full swing, the Association of Young Writers being aided by volunteers from the newly-formed and already vigorous D. H. Lawrence Society, which has three district councillors as members, and by students and school children. The top floor has been let as a flat and the ground floor is to be a Lawrence museum which may already be open to the public by the time this book appears.

It looks, then, as if attitudes are changing and that Eastwood is coming to accept Lawrence as 'a good thing'. It may never become a second Stratford, but it already gets a sprinkling of visitors from overseas—especially from the United States, where a flourishing D. H. Lawrence Society has already contributed to the Garden Street restoration—and there is no reason why it should not develop quite an important tourist trade. And the tourists, when they have looked at the four Lawrence homes—97 Lynn Croft Road, the 'semi' to which the family moved in 1902, was the last one—might also have a look at the parish church of St Mary, an admirable modern building, replacing one burnt down in 1963, married to the original tower that Lawrence knew.

The countryside around is very much 'Lawrence country', particularly if you follow the Mansfield road, the A608. Just below the Sun Inn, itself a listed building, is Eastwood Hall, another listed building now an area headquarters of the National Coal Board. It was the probable setting for Lawrence's last play, *Touch and Go*. His father, Arthur Lawrence, was born in the cottage in the quarry hole by the disused level crossing at Brinsley. 'But my uncle built the cottage over again—all spoilt,' Lawrence wrote to Rolf Gardiner. The headstocks of the old pit where Arthur worked have recently been taken down to be re-erected at the colliery museum at Lound Hall in the north of the county.

Just beyond the old crossing, the A608 joins for a short distance the A613, which is by far the most attractive route from Nottingham into the Lawrence country. It leaves Nottingham by way of Nuthall, where the M 1 now strides across what were once the grounds of Nuthall Temple, that glorious descendant of Palladio's Villa Rotonda, ingloriously demolished in 1929. Beyond Watnall Cantelupe—too suburbanized to live up to the promise of its name—it leaves suburbia behind at Watnall Chaworth, where a bend in the road suddenly reveals the fifteenth-century tower of Greasley church peeping up above a belt of trees. It is a charming view, owing much to eighteenth-century landscaping, but slightly marred in a way that would have roused Lawrence's wrath by an obtrusive fence that has replaced a roadside hedge all the way down the hill and up the other side. It may sound a slight carp, but when the beauty lies, as it does here, in small-scale scenery, the slightest bit of insensitivity can strike a jarring note. Fortunately, there is nothing to jar at Greasley. Not that there is a great deal of anything there; just a small cluster of buildings on a leafy hill-top site; a nineteenth-century restored church with a splendid fifteenth-century tower rising above the beech trees and next to it a large farmhouse with traces of a castle in the outbuildings standing above what was once a moat, forming a charming group. Greasley Castle was in fact a fortified manor built, or rebuilt and fortified, about 1340 by the wealthy Nicholas Cantelupe, member of a family who had already produced a Lord Chancellor and a Bishop of Worcester. Both the wealth and castle crumbled away during the stormy Middle Ages, but excavations were carried out in 1901, which must have been around the time that young Lawrence was spending some of his 'happiest days . . . haymaking in the fields just opposite the south side of Greasley church—bottom of Watnall Hill—adjoining the vicarage'. Jesse Chambers' father (Miriam Lievers' father in *Sons and Lovers*) rented the fields. They are the scene of the short story *Love Among the Haystacks*, but in this the farmer's name has changed to Wooley. 'These two fields were four miles from the home farm. But they had been in the hands of the Wooleys for several generations, therefore the father kept them on, and everyone looked forward to the hay harvest at Greasley, it was a kind of picnic. They brought dinner and tea in the milk float which the father drove over in the morning. The lads and labourers cycled. Off and on, the harvest lasted for a fortnight . . . the high road from Alfreton to Nottingham ran at the foot of the fields.'

As it does today. Nothing has changed. Nor has it at Moorgreen, except that the Ram Inn has increased in size and is probably across the road from the site that Lawrence described in *The White Peacock*. But Moorgreen Reservoir, just along the road north of the little village, is still unmistakably the Nethermere of the same novel; and very lovely it is. One may be bitterly opposed to the construction of reservoirs; grumble, quite rightly, about the loss of good agricultural land, the felling of trees, the general desecration of beautiful countryside; and yet one must admit that they often add something aesthetically satisfying to the landscape. Certainly, where parking space is provided, motorists will sit for hours just gazing at the water. Moorgreen has no such provision. It was built in the canal age, to provide water for the Nottingham Canal, and it is not easy to find convenient parking space off the road. If it was it would certainly attract swarms of motorists, for it is undeniably beautiful. Approached from the north, with High Park woods rising to nearly 600 feet from its shores, it reminds one of a Scottish loch. The view from the south is only slightly less pleasing. To the right, you catch a glimpse of Beauvale House, to the left is Lambelose House (Highclose in *The White Peacock*, but it turns up in various Lawrence novels under different names), the home of the Barbers (called Crich in *Women in Love*), then the local colliery owners.

Just before you come to Moorgreen Reservoir, close to the Ram Inn in fact, an unsignposted lane wanders off to the right, describes a vague triangle in linking up several scattered farms, and eventually finds its way back to the main road at Watnall Chaworth. It is worth following this lane from Moorgreen for a mile or so to find the remains of Beauvale Priory. They lie to the left of the lane behind a farmhouse from which permission to view the ruins should be obtained. There is not much left; just the Prior's lodgings and a wall of the church, with some less readily identifiable portions now embodied in farm buildings. It perhaps requires less effort of the imagination to picture Beauvale (the beautiful valley) as it was in 1343 when the first Prior and 12 monks founded the house and settled down to live their austere lives under the strict Carthusian rules, than the relatively prosperous house it had become—sending out monks as vicars to neighbouring parishes and others to work the coal at Selston—when Henry VIII's commissioner, 'the insolent and pompous Dr Legh,' as a contemporary described him, closed it in 1538.

But what comes back into the mind at Beauvale, as one mounts the crumbling flight of external stone steps and peers in through the open doorway on the first floor at a still handsome fireplace and a spiral staircase in the far corner of the room, is the heroism of two men who occupied this room at various times. One was the last Prior but one. His name, by an improbable coincidence, was Lawrence, Robert Lawrence. He defied Henry VIII and died for it. This followed the Act of Supremacy of 1534. The Carthusians refused to recognise Henry as Supreme Head of the Church of England. Robert Lawrence, with John Houghton, a former Prior of Beauvale who had become Prior of the London Charterhouse, went along with the Prior of Axeholme in Lincolnshire to see Thomas Cromwell, then Lord Privy Seal, to explain their reasons, but Cromwell refused to receive them. Instead, he ordered them to the Tower, and kept them there for six weeks, intending to break their spirit. In this he failed. The three Priors still refused to take the Oath of Supremacy. Cromwell then ordered them to be tried by a jury on a peculiar charge of 'verbal treason'. The jury sat on 28 May 1535, and at the end of the day refused to condemn the prisoners because they were not acting 'maliciously'. At this Cromwell flew into a rage and threatened the jury, who eventually weakened and passed the required verdict of guilty. A week later the three Priors were taken to Tyburn and brutally tortured before execution, after each man in turn had refused a free pardon. Sir Thomas More, watching them leave the Tower on their last journey, said they went 'as cheerfully to their deaths as bridegrooms to their marriage'.

There is a pleasant walk through High Park Woods to Felley Mill

Farm, *The White Peacock* farm, according to Lawrence, and the ruins of the mill itself, but the motorist can approach it by taking the rather stony lane (now called Felley Lane South) almost opposite the junction of the A608 and the A613. To the right of this lane lies Haggs Farm, the old home of the Chambers family, though in fact the house has been rebuilt since then. 'That was Miriam's farm—where I got my first incentive to write.' The farm, so important in literary history, is private, of course, as it always has been. But you can take a footpath from the ford by the mill, a charmingly nostalgic spot, 'and go on uphill, up the rough deserted pasture—on past Annesley Kennels— long empty—on to Annesley again. That's the country of my heart.'

Annesley can also be reached by following the A608 when it swings eastward to leave the A613 at Underwood. Just beyond the last houses of Friesland, virtually an extension of Underwood, a drive on the right runs down to Felley Priory. This is a private house embodying some fragments of the building that Ralph Britto of Annesley founded for the Augustinian Canons in 1156. The house was badly damaged by fire a few years ago when its owner, Mr C. A. M. Oakes died after saving one of his domestic staff. Just over the hill where the road crosses the M.1, the wall of Annesley Hall begins. Behind it stand the ruins of All Saints, Annesley, 'the mouldering church which stands high on a bank by the roadside just where the trees tunnel the darkness and the gloom of the highway startles the traveller at noon. Great trees growing on the banks suddenly fold over everything at this point in the swinging road, and in the obscurity rots the Hall church, black and melancholy above the shrinking head of the traveller'. That was how Lawrence saw it, and Pevsner, in a similar melancholy mood, agreed that it was 'not a picturesque ruin, just an utterly neglected derelict building'. For me, I must admit, it has a certain romantic charm.

But Annesley is perhaps more closely linked with Byron than with Lawrence. Here one is at the boundary of the lands of the two writers and on the edge of the forest which must be left to the next chapter. The tourist may either return to Nottingham along the M1 or go back to Underwood and explore the country inside the first loop of the Erewash from its source just south of Kirkby-in-Ashfield.

This is rather odd, uneven country, in which the characteristics of the whole valley seem to be accentuated; a stretch of short, steep hills

14. (opposite, above) *Newstead Abbey, with memorial to Byron's dog Boatswain on the raised lawn*

15. (below) *Fourteenth-century gatehouse of Worksop Priory*

and narrow valleys, industrial and rural, ugly and quite beautiful within a matter of yards. Round Selston (Lawrence's Selby), Westwood, Bagthorpe and Underwood, coal was worked very early, and again in the nineteenth century. It is the nineteenth century that has left its mark most prominently, as names like Alma and Inkerman make clear on the map, but there are occasional much older buildings, like Wansley Hall at Westwood, and a few farmhouses and cottages. Sometimes a nineteenth-century shell hides a much older interior, as in Selston Church, where an enlargement of 1889 left the thirteenth-century church within untouched and well worth visiting. So, for different reasons, is Pye Hill No. 2 Colliery at Underwood, tucked away behind modern housing almost opposite the school where Jessie Chambers could have begun her education. One does not expect a pit to be beautiful and this one is not, but it is no longer the eyesore that it was 30 years or so ago. The gaunt headstocks are now cocooned in concrete and the new offices are as bright and cheerful as a modern school. It would be foolish to suggest that we are winning the war against ugliness, but here is a sign that we are at least winning a few battles.

Not far away is a hill from which one can count seven church spires sticking up, often very prettily, and probably just as many colliery tips, much less prettily; the Erewash Valley is like that, but at least a good deal of the smoke of a decade or so ago has cleared away and many tips have been levelled. You notice this if you stand at the top of Jubilee Hill, where the A613 from Selston suddenly drops into an abyss that has the Erewash at the bottom and Derbyshire on the far bank. It always struck me as being odd when I was a boy that from Nottinghamshire, that was supposed to be flat, you looked down into Derbyshire, that was supposed to be hilly. Not having been that way for some years, I went back half expecting to find the steepness of the hill a figment of childhood imagination, but in fact the gradient turned out to be one in five, a stiff enough climb for anyone entering Nottinghamshire that way. Certainly, it would make an impressive introduction to the Lawrence Country.

16. (opposite, above left) *Brass to Dame Margaret Mering, d.* 1419, *East Markham Church*

17. (right) *Norman font in All Saints, West Markham*

18. (below) *The monument to William Huntingdon, 'ship carpenter', in West Stockwith Church*

CHAPTER FOUR

The Forest

Sherwood Forest once covered one fifth of Nottinghamshire. Today, though much reduced in size, it is still large enough to deserve two chapters to itself. To demand it in fact, because of the change of scenery that occurs near enough to the A617 road to make that a convenient boundary line between the Dukeries to the north and the remainder of the Forest to the south.

This southern section may not live up to the popular idea of a forest, but then it has not done so for several hundred years. It is true that Major Rooke, an historian of the Forest, wrote in 1799 that a friend's father, born a century earlier, had claimed to remember 'one continuous wood from Mansfield to Nottingham'. But old men forget, and even then a great deal of the Forest, particularly at its edges, was no longer particularly thickly wooded. Indeed that pioneer cartographer of roads, John Ogilby, had shown the southern half of Sherwood to be afforested in 1675 to much the same extent and in much the same places as it is today. A great deal of clearance had already taken place before then, but it is doubtful if this part had ever been densely wooded throughout. There must always have been between the belts of woodland the great open spaces implied in the suffix *-field* in Mansfield, and the Ashfield that included Sutton and Kirkby. A forest was, as the Elizabethan John Manwood began his classic definition, 'a certaine Territorie of wooddy grounds and fruitfull pastures . . .'. That, with a few collieries thrown in, is what Sherwood is today.

From Nottingham three main roads now lead into the Forest Two go to Mansfield, the other, the Old North Road, to Bawtry and on into the East Riding of Yorkshire. Each has much to offer, and if the westernmost, the A611, has the least beauty it has enough of the Nottinghamshire contrasts to make it worth following.

Its early stages through the north-western suburbs of Nottingham and the industrialised valley of the Leen are uninspiring, though Bulwell on Tuesdays has a busy little street market that adds a touch of gaiety in the surrounding drabness and could give more if the stallholders followed the Norwich example of using brightly coloured awnings. Farther along the road some welcome brightness is added to the approaches to Hucknall by the Sherwood Zoo. Opened in 1968, it is still fairly small but has already built up a good reputation for the presentation and maintenance of its collection.

Hucknall needs all the brightness it can get. Overshadowed by its coalmines, it remains, as J. B. Firth described it in his *Highways and Byways in Nottinghamshire in 1916*, 'a dreary mining town of depressing ugliness'. It is doing its best, however, to be less depressing. There are a few modern buildings which, if not beautiful, are at least ugly in a different way, and the council has provided a most pleasing precinct with seats where tired shoppers can rest their feet and gaze across the market square at such Victoriana as the public library that looks like one of Emett's crazier railway stations, a statue of Byron in a niche above the Co-op, and, unexpectedly, a large church with a handsome tower standing in a churchyard that has stepped out of a Victorian picture-postcard.

The church, enlarged, rebuilt and restored in the 1870s and 1880s to keep pace with the growth of the parish, is a place of pilgrimage. These pilgrims come, usually, not so much to admire the excellent timber south porch that was erected in 1320 when the vicar was Thomas Torkard, last local member of a family who had been lords of the manor for 150 years and whose name was only dropped officially from the town's name about 1970, when Hucknall Torkard became Hucknall; nor the fourteenth-century font, nor even the 27 attractive stained-glass windows by Kempe, but to gaze at a slab of marble set in the chancel floor. It bears a simple, effective inscription: BYRON, and, underneath, *Born January 22nd, 1788, Died April 19th, 1824*. The whole inscription is surmounted by a laurel wreath, the sole prize for those victorious in the Greek Olympic Games. On the south wall of the chancel is a memorial tablet to the poet, put there by his half-sister Augusta Mary Leigh. Just east of the lectern is the door leading to the family vault, now sealed, where 27 members of the family, from the wife of the first Lord Byron in the mid-seventeenth century to the poet's daughter Augusta Ada, who married Lord

Lovelace, in the nineteenth century. Among them is the poet himself.

It is necessary to stress this because a strange tradition grew up that Byron's body was not there. The rumour became so strong that one Hucknall incumbent, Canon T. G. Barber, vicar for 39 years, decided to see for himself. With utmost secrecy, to keep away sightseers, the vault was opened on 15 June, 1938. What he found he later described in a book, *Byron and where he is buried*, extracts from which are printed in the pleasantly written church guidebook. On reaching the coffin he found the lid loose and the leaden case within cut open. 'Someone had deliberately opened the coffin . . . . Had the body itself been removed? . . . . Reverently, very reverently, I raised the lid, and before my eyes lay the embalmed body of Byron in as perfect condition as when it was placed in the coffin one hundred and fourteen years ago. His features and hair easily recognizable from the portraits with which I was so familiar. The serene, almost happy expression on his face made a profound impression on me. The feet and ankles were uncovered, and I was able to establish the fact that his lameness had been that of the right foot.'

Hucknall is very much Byron country. Sir Ralf de Buron held land there at the time of Domesday, long before the Torkards arrived. Byron is a name that springs readily to Hucknall shop fronts. There is a Byron Cinema; there used to be a football club called Hucknall Byron. Such pride is understandable; the ancestral home, Newstead Abbey, is a mere two miles away as the crow flies, though twice that by road.

But the townsfolk have a soft spot for other natives. One, Ben Caunt, the prizefighter whose contests with Bendigo have already been mentioned, is buried in the churchyard. The other is Eric Coates, son of a much loved local doctor and a Welsh born mother of musical tastes and skill. The birthplace, occupied now by another doctor, bears a plaque commemorating the birth on 27 August 1886. It was there at the age of six that Eric Coates demanded—and obtained—his first violin, and started out on the road that was to take him to the Queen's Hall as principal viola player in Sir Henry J. Wood's Queen's Hall Orchestra. But, slightly reluctantly, he gave up playing as his fame as a composer of light music grew. When he died in 1957 two of his pieces had become signature tunes of popular radio programmes. His *Covent Garden*, from the *Knightsbridge Suite* (1933) introduced

In Town Tonight each Saturday to millions of listeners; *Sleepy Lagoon* (1930) continues each week to salute the guest whom Roy Plomley is about to maroon on some heat-soaked Pacific island with his *Desert Island Discs*.

It would be hard to imagine a greater contrast between the grim reality of Eric Coates' native town and the romantic island of his musical imagination. Yet the transformation when you leave Hucknall behind is hardly less striking. Before you have passed the last of its houses you have the Forest around you. It is not perhaps quite the forest you have imagined; shafts of sunlight do not peer romantically through the thick leaves of oak and beech into romantic glades. What trees there are are mainly conifers; for the most part this a stretch of open country, its sandy soil lying under a cover of bracken except for patches where the undergrowth has yielded to the energies of generations of agricultural improvers. It is a fresh, invigorating landscape that stretches away on either side of the A611 almost into Mansfield. There are no ancient settlements along the road, the only built up area being the late-nineteenth century colliery village of New Annesley, much less displeasing than many of its kind with a pleasant church by T. G. Jackson in 1874 (rebuilt after a fire in 1908) that contains a Norman font and a sixteenth-century monument transferred from the ruined church in Annesley Park that I mentioned in the last chapter.

This is a pleasant main road, as main roads go, but unless you are a golfer anxious to make the acquaintance of the famous Hollinwell course, you might do better to turn eastward on to the B6011 on the northern outskirts of Hucknall. This is not only the quickest way to reach Newstead Abbey but it also leads through Linby and Papplewick, which are well worth seeing in their own right. In fact the first view of Linby offers one of the most amazing of those transformation scenes that seem to me so characteristic of the county.

When you leave the main road you seem to be turning your back on the Forest again. A colliery looms up on the right; you are conscious of a scattering of shacks as you bump over two level crossings, and then, quite suddenly, you are—if not in fairyland—at least in as passable an imitation as you could expect to find after the industrial squalor of the Leen Valley.

Linby may not be quite a Thornton Dale or a Lower Slaughter—the red brick between-wars council houses near the church are an unfortunate intrusion that is out of context with the rest of the village—but it has some of the same characteristics: a stream running along the village street, wide grass verges, a pleasant looking inn and handsome houses standing back from the road and built mainly of local limestone. 'One of the prettiest villages on the north side of Nottingham', is Pevsner's fairly guarded comment. It is also one of the few predominantly stone-built villages in the whole county. For good measure there are stone crosses at each end of the village and a most interesting church. The purpose of the crosses is uncertain. It has been suggested that they marked the boundary of Sherwood Forest. This seems unlikely, but they may possibly have marked a boundary between wards. The cross at the west end of the village is much the older. Its seven steps are medieval, though its shaft was restored in the nineteenth century. The other dates from the seventeenth century. The church is charming, It has battlements, pinnacles and gargoyles and a Norman south door. Its architectural history must be something of a packman's puzzle, because the exterior of the fabric reveals traces of doorways and windows that have been blocked off, probably at different periods. The churchyard is charmingly kept, neither excessively wild nor aggressively tidy, but, grimly, it has 42 graves of apprentice children to remind us that Linby was once an industrial village in which life was apt to be short and brutish.

A good deal of local legend surrounds these graves and the conditions at Robinson's Mills where these pauper children worked. There are usually said to be 163, as well as mounds in fields elsewhere that are asserted, most improbably, to be communal graves of other apprentices. Recent researchers have tended to play down these wilder stories. All that can be said for certain is that the cotton empire of the Robinson family around Linby and Papplewick employed a good deal of child labour; that the lives of these children were no more enjoyable than in any other mill in the late eighteenth century and that some of them died young. Even those bare facts are pitiful enough without any further elaboration.

However bad they may have been as employers it cannot be denied that George Robinson and his sons, John and James, were remarkably enterprising men. Their chief claim to a place in national industrial history lies in their being the first to use steam power to drive a textile factory. The pioneer Boulton and Watt 10 horse-power steam engine began work in February 1786 in one of the numerous mills they had built around Papplewick during the previous decade. But perhaps even more remarkable than their quickness to grasp the possibilities of steam power was their ability to make use of the infant Leen to drive the earlier machinery. A few years earlier Richard Arkwright had rejected the lower Leen as unsuitable for his purpose and had moved his factory from Nottingham to find swifter streams in Derbyshire. Yet somehow the Robinsons managed by skilful engineering to persuade this narrow, slow-moving stream to do a substantial job of work at least reasonably well, even if the early purchase of a steam engine suggests that it may have caused some anxieties. The remnants of their waterworks and some of their eight mills can still be seen to the west of the Bulwell-Papplewick road, as can two rows of cottages, known as Grange Cottages, that are the sole survivors of the Robinsons' mill village. But the most interesting extant building stands a little to the north, between Linby and Papplewick. This is the Castle Mill, a pleasantly eccentric piece of industrial architecture with two battlemented towers on the north side facing the road, built, David Smith suggests, 'to keep up with the Byrons', which seems quite likely as the rear is completely functional. It is now an unusual but quite attractive private house, a rare example of a mill being transformed into a semi-stately house (the four storey building being a good deal bigger than it seems at first glance), though it is a pity that the original pointed Gothic-style windows were replaced during the conversion. But we must be thankful that this memorial to the Robinson cotton empire that grew, flourished and faded away in the space of half a century is likely to endure, even though it is fairly certainly not the building that housed the historic steam engine.

'Papplewick is not as pretty as Linby', a lady in Linby told me. She may be right, largely because Papplewick has fewer stone buildings and no streams in its main street, but it is 'the nearest run thing', as the Duke of Wellington said of Waterloo. Papplewick has some most pleasing buildings and one of the most attractive—and least conveniently—sited churches in the county. It lies on the edge of a park at the end of a long, excruciatingly narrow lane which must test the ability of drivers of wedding cars. But the setting is superb;

woods stretching right down to the churchyard from Papplewick Hall on two sides, open parkland on the others. It is very much a big house church. It is impossible to get round on to the north side of the church; a notice on a fence warns that it is private property. In a moment of irritation at finding the door locked and no information about the whereabouts of the key, you wonder if the church was built for the worship of God or of the Honourable Frederick Montagu, whose initials are carved over the porch. But it is impossible to retain that mood for long in such idyllic surroundings, and after all Montagu did rebuild his church at a time when equally wealthy men were allowing theirs to rot, and planted a great many trees hereabouts, naming his plantations after successful contemporary admirals. It is difficult, too, to be annoyed by a man whose tomb in the churchyard is a plain, six-legged table of stone with a simple inscription. If you ignored the ugly railings around it, you could take it for an old kitchen table dragged outside for a picnic.

Montagu, a Lord of the Treasury at the time of the unfortunate Fox-North Coalition of 1783, rebuilt the church in 1795, five years before his death. He sensibly left the fourteenth-century west tower standing and had the fabric built in the Gothic style to match—or nearly so; he, or his architect, could not resist the rather impressive pediment, unmistakably late eighteenth century, over the pointed very Gothic arch of the south porch. A particularly interesting feature of the porch is the inscribed slabs built into it that must have adorned the coffin lids of forest workers, and there are more of these in the nave. One has the sling, bow and arrow of a forester, a second the knife of a woodward, two more have the bellows of ironworkers, who presumably worked in the forest smithy. Above the door are two small Norman figures; one is said to be St James. But inside the church it is Squire Montagu again who catches the eye. At the east end of the gallery that runs the length of the north wall is his private pew, complete with fireplace. One squire used to bring the sermon to an abrupt conclusion by rattling the fire-irons when he had heard enough, or so I was told by a man who was tidying up the churchyard under the shade of the old yew tree which is 14 feet in circumference. A more recent squire, one of the Chadburns of the Mansfield brewery firm, has completely repewed the church since the last war.

You get a fairly distant view of the house that Montagu built in 1787 as you drive on towards Newstead. Tradition says that he employed the Adam brothers as architects and certainly Papplewick Hall looks handsome enough in its restrained way to have been their handiwork. Two of Montagu's literary friends are commemorated in the grounds. There is an urn in memory of Thomas Gray, of *Elegy* fame, of whom Dr Johnson said 'he was dull in company, dull in his closet, dull everywhere', and a Tuscan temple to William Mason, who wrote more flatteringly in a biography of Gray.

Opposite the Hall gates a public footpath labelled to Larch Farm leads to the gates of Newstead Abbey and on through pinewoods to such fascinating places as the Sheppard Stone, commemorating the early nineteenth-century murder of a Miss Sheppard of Papplewick, and Thieves Wood, but the less energetic may stay carbound and still get very near to these places after a short but lovely drive, though the last stretch to Newstead is on the busy A60 Mansfield-Nottingham road. Facing the Abbey gates is the Hutt Hotel, once a coaching inn and later, for a time in the nineteenth century, the residence of the Abbey chaplain. Just by the entrance lodge is the celebrated Pilgrim Oak, one of the few ancient trees on the estate to escape the frenzied hatchet of the fifth Lord Byron, 'the wicked Lord' who was the poet's great uncle. A mile-long drive then brings you to what the Ordnance Survey map calls, with strict accuracy and a refusal to bow to public opinion, Newstead Priory.

It never was an abbey. Newstead, 'the new place' (Novo Loco in Sherwode), was established by Henry II between 1165 and 1173 as a priory of Augustinian Canons, the black canons because of their sombre habit. But as almost everyone knows it as Newstead Abbey, I propose to conform. Its history as a religious house was comparatively uneventful. Starting with the endowment of the church and town of Papplewick, it gradually acquired other land in the area, played host to a succession of kings from John in 1201 to Henry VII, and for one night in 1530 to Cardinal Wolsey on his last journey from York to Leicester, and was dissolved in 1539. A year later its endowments were granted for £800 to Sir John Byron of Colwick, 'Little Sir John with the Great Beard', whose ghostly figure reading a book in the library is one of the quieter ghosts that are reputed to frequent this much haunted house.

The early Byrons tended to be belligerent. For the first few centuries after their arrival from Normandy as de Burons they worked off their surplus energy quite legitimately in battle. Six or seven of them (the records are imprecise) fought at Edgehill for their king, who created the current Sir John the first Baron Byron of Rochdale. His brother Richard, who succeeded to the title, commanded the Royalist garrison in the siege of Newark Castle, and later entertained Charles II. The third and fourth lords apparently lived less eventful lives, but the fifth, 'the wicked Lord', or 'Devil Byron', made up for this with considerable gusto.

As a young man he had the reputation for wildness and extravagance bordering on madness, but it was in 1765, 29 years after he had succeeded to the title, that he created a stir by killing his neighbour, cousin and friend William Chaworth of Annesley in a duel. The incident occurred in London, at the Star and Garter Tavern in Pall Mall, where a number of Nottinghamshire gentlemen met regularly for convivial evenings. On this occasion an after dinner discussion about the game laws became heated. Chaworth took a hard line on poachers; Byron insisted that the best way to preserve game was to take no precautions. The argument became intense. Chaworth said he had more game on five acres of his than Byron had on his entire estates. Byron was prepared to bet 100 guineas against this. The other guests tried to take the heat out of the argument, but after a time there was another flare up, ending with what sounded like a challenge from Chaworth, which was certainly not immediately taken up, but which abruptly ended that particular discussion. A few minutes later, Chaworth paid his bill and left. Byron followed and overtook him on the stairs. Another challenge was given, though by whom was never established. They continued on to the next floor where a waiter found them an empty room and a candle, and left them briefly until he was summoned by a bell. He found Chaworth wounded, and sent for the landlord, who immediately called a doctor. But Chaworth died shortly after, though not before he had given a brief account of what happened, from which it seemed that Byron drew first but that they both made thrusts.

Three months later the House of Lords, who only five years earlier had sentenced to death a Leicestershire peer, Earl Ferrers, for the murder of his steward, took a more lenient view. They found Byron guilty of manslaughter, but by using an ancient statute that 'peers are in all cases, where clergy is allowed, to be dismissed without burning in the hand, loss of inheritance or corruption of blood' they were able to set him free on payment of costs that did in fact lose him a good deal of his inheritance.

He had, according to Horace Walpole, who visited Newstead in 1760 already 'lost large sums and paid part in old oaks, five thousand pounds' worth of which had been cut near the house. In recompense he has built two baby forts . . . and planted a handful of Scotch firs, that look like ploughboys dressed in old family liveries for a public day!' He did little in his last lonely, malevolent years at Newstead to restore his fortune. Even the destruction of almost all the remaining trees seems to have been less an attempt to raise cash than an act of mindless vandalism as his annihilation of all his deer undoubtedly was. That the Abbey itself was allowed to fall into decay owed more to the hatred of the son to whom it was to pass than to false economy.

As it turned out, the son died first. The new heir was a great-nephew, George Gordon Byron, the future poet, 'that brat in Aberdeen' as the wicked Lord described the small boy he never met. He was the son of 'mad Jack' Byron, not to be confused with his father 'foul weather Jack' Byron, the wicked Lord's brother, an able and popular admiral who earned a reputation for running into gales at sea. 'Mad Jack' was a Guards officer who created his own storms, mainly financial. To weather these he employed his only marketable assets, good looks and charm. He seduced the Marchioness of Caernarvon and then married her after her divorce. She gave him two daughters, of whom only Augusta survived, and an income of £4,000 a year which died with her. Recovering quickly from his loss, Jack Byron fell in love with the fortune of £24,000 belonging to Catherine Gordon of Gight, a descendant of Scottish kings, and persuaded her to marry him. They lived for a time in London, where their only son was born on 23 January 1788, before moving first to France and then to Aberdeen in an effort to keep costs down and creditors at a distance. But before long Jack Byron found it expedient to leave his wife and baby and return to France where he died in 1791, 'penniless, poxed and unrepentant', as one writer has it.

From this unsatisfactory home background—a father whom, perhaps fortunately, he never knew and a moody, snobbish mother, of whom he wrote at 16, 'The more I see of her the more my dislike of her augments'—sprang George Gordon Byron, who became Sixth Baron Byron of Rochdale on the death of the wicked Lord in 1798. Apart from having unfortunate parents, Byron also was deeply sensitive about his lameness, probably caused by some muscular paralysis, though it did not stop him from playing cricket for Harrow, boxing, fencing or swimming the Hellespont. But a psychologist would probably attribute much of Byron's subsequent unhappiness to these early misfortunes.

However, what we are concerned with here must only be Byron's residence at Newstead. This did not begin until 1808. In that year Byron came down from Cambridge—and Lord Grey de Ruthyn, who had been using the Abbey virtually as a shooting box, gave up his tenancy after some mysterious quarrel with his landlord. Byron, though 'cursedly dipped' in debt, had to spend much money to make the house even reasonably habitable as a country residence where he could give small bachelor parties. These seem to have been no more than the usual high-spirited adolescent affairs typical of undergraduates then, and now, but popular legend has given them a more sinister twist. There has been talk of orgies and black magic, but an old Harrow school friend, William Harness who stayed three weeks at Newstead said 'that nothing in the shape of riot or excess occurred while I was there. The only other visitor was Dr Hodgson, the translator of *Juvenal*, and nothing could be more quiet and regular than the course of our days'. Admittedly Harness's visit was in 1811, by which time Byron had reached manhood and may have been taking life more soberly. There certainly had been a skull cup—said to be the skull of a monk—used for drinking toasts, and apparently buried by a later owner. But Byron's own account of what went on—as given to John Murray, his publisher in a letter of 1820—was probably true. 'We were a company of seven or eight, with an occasional neighbour or so for visitors, and used to sit up late in our friars' dresses, drinking burgundy, claret, champagne, and what not, out of the skull-cup and all sorts of glasses, and buffooning all round the house in our conventual garments.' It sounds pretty harmless, a pale imitation of the Hell Fire Club's activities at Medmenham Abbey half a century earlier. Late hours were kept—two or three in the morning was bedtime—and a visitor who rose before noon occasioned comment;

there was some wildish pistol shooting inside a mansion whose other hazards included a bear and a wolf as pets, in addition to Byron's bloodhounds, but probably nothing much that could not be covered by the harmless word 'buffooning'.

Life at Newstead was not always as happy for Byron. It was there in 1803, while staying as a guest of his tenant Lord Grey de Ruthyn, that he fell violently in love with Mary Chaworth, the charming 17-year-old great-niece of the man who died at the hands of Byron's great-uncle. It was not quite a Romeo and Juliet affair, as the family friendship seems to have survived the duel, but it was nearly as intense, nearly as short-lived, and, for Byron, nearly as tragic. She was older than Byron, more mature, and already engaged to John Musters of Colwick, a superb rider to hounds who was subsequently to bring unhappiness to his wife as well as to the foxes of south Nottinghamshire. 'Do you think I could care for that lame boy?' she is supposed to have said in Byron's hearing. The double wound went deep. Not long after he went to live at Newstead his Newfoundland dog Boatswain died and was buried near the site of the altar of the Abbey Church under an ornate monument whose inscription refers to one Who possessed Beauty without Vanity, Strength without Insolence, Courage without Ferocity, And all the Virtues of Man without his Vices. Three years later Byron's mother, who had lived at the Abbey since 1809, died there before he could reach her from London. He refused to attend the funeral, spending the time of the service sparring with a servant.

Memories of these events did not shake Byron's genuine affection for Newstead. When he went there he was so hard up that he was contemplating, in surprisingly modern words, 'marrying a golden dolly or blowing my brains out'. Yet he refused, at least at first, to consider selling Newstead. 'Newstead and I', he wrote to his mother, 'stand or fall together. I have now lived on the spot, I have fixed my heart upon it, and no pressure, present or future, shall induce me to barter the last vestage of our inheritance.' He repeated this determination a month or two afterwards, adding 'were my head as grey and defenceless as the arch of the Priory I would abide by this resolution'. Eighteen months later he was writing from Athens, 'my only tie to England is Newstead, and that once gone neither interest nor inclination lead me northward'. But he had to sell in November 1817 about the same time that he was forced to break another resolution and accept payment for his writing. He was then living in exile in Italy after the failure of his marriage, and even to get there, and to escape his more pressing creditors in London, he had to borrow money. The £94,000 he received from Colonel Thomas Wildman, an old Harrow schoolfellow, for the sale of Newstead, ended his financial worries. The last seven years before he was struck down by illness were the most affluent of his life.

The sale also brought new life to Newstead. Wildman immediately tackled an extensive restoration that went on for about 12 years, and the mansion you see today is largely his work, the succession of later owners having made few alterations. From 1828 he employed as his architect John Shaw of London, designer of St Dunstan's in the West, who created the Sussex Tower but built into it some parts of an original Norman doorway on the ground floor. The tower, named after George IV's brother the Duke of Sussex, to whom Wildman served as equerry, is the most prominent feature of the battlemented mansion.

Newstead always strikes me as being rather a gloomy house, but it is well worth seeing, of course, not only for its Byron relics and associations but also for its architectural interest. And somehow it does harmonize with the ruins of the old Abbey it adjoins, 'an exceptionally perfect example of a late thirteenth-century church front', as Pevsner says. It is a glorious spectacle, but a melancholy one too. Standing in front of the ruin you are reminded of Canto 13 of *Don Juan*:

> *A mighty window, hollow in the centre,*
> *Shorn of its glass of a thousand colourings,*
> *Through which the deepened glories once could enter,*
> *Streaming from off the Sun lime Seraph's wings,*
> *Now yawns all desolate: now loud, now fainter,*
> *The gale sweeps through its fretwork, and oft sings,*
> *The owl his anthem, where silenced quire*
> *Lie with their hallelujahs quenched like fire.*

Standing below that yawning window it is easy to understand why Newstead is alleged to be haunted and to believe especially in the Black Friar who is said to appear when something unpleasant is about to happen to the head of the household.

When an heir is born, he's heard to mourn
And when aught is to befall
That ancient line, in the pale moonshine
He walks from hall to hall.

Byron said he saw him a month before his own ill-fated marriage to Annabella Milbanke, but that may have been moonshine of another sort.

Newstead has had other famous visitors besides the Black Friar. One was Dr Livingstone. He was a friend of Mr F. W. Webb, himself an explorer, who bought the house on Wildman's death, and filled it with stuffed animals. Since 1931, Newstead has belonged to Nottingham Corporation, to whom it was presented by Sir Julian Cahn. The house is open to the public daily from Easter to the end of September. The splendid grounds are open all through the year, forts and all.

Four, mainly attractive, miles north of Newstead Abbey lies Mansfield, the county's second largest town. It is not now perhaps the 'praty market town' that Leland saw in the reign of Henry VIII, but nor is it the ugly colliery town that most strangers seem to expect. The rapid growth of its population—from 6,000 to 50,000—in the nineteenth century was caused by mining development, but there is not now a single colliery inside the borough boundary, though there are plenty just outside. Its industries are now much more diverse and less obtrusive, and if the suggestion of an ex-mayor that it had a future as a holiday centre may have been the product of wishful thinking it was not quite as wild an idea as his derisive critics seemed to think. It would make a quite reasonable centre for an exploration of the Dukeries, with the Peak not far to the west. The snag would be that, as Celia Fiennes noted three centuries ago, 'there is nothing remarkable here', except perhaps an unfortunately sited and prominent railway viaduct that she did not see and a splendidly spacious market place a few yards away that may have been enlarged since her visit. It is a pity that this quite pleasant town that has had a market since 1277—though it did not become a municipal borough until 1891— should have so few distinguished buildings, though its locally quarried white and red sandstone has added distinction to such buildings elsewhere as the Houses of Parliament and St Pancras Station.

89

But Mansfield has produced its famous men. One was Archbishop Sterne, who as chaplain to William Laud, attended him at his execution. Another was Robert Dodsley, who was later to publish *Tristram Shandy*, by the Archbishop's grandson, Laurence Sterne.

Dodsley, son of a master at Queen Elizabeth's Grammar School, Mansfield, was born in 1704. Originally apprenticed to a stockinger, he ran away and became a footman. Having literary leanings he quickly accepted the old advice about writing on what one knows and turned out work in both prose and verse on life below stairs. This attracted the attention of Alexander Pope, who first helped him to get a short play, *The Toy Shop*, produced with success at Covent Garden and then lent him £100 to open a bookshop in Pall Mall. There, as was the custom of the time, he published books as well as selling them. An early venture was a book called *London* from an unknown writer named Samuel Johnson, whom he paid ten guineas. He later gave him £100 for *Rasselas*, and then generously added another £25 when the second edition appeared, as well as suggesting that Johnson might try his hand at a dictionary. Thomas Gray was another Dodsley discovery; a profitable one after an initial failure with *An Ode on a Distant Prospect of Eton College*. The *Elegy* was much more successful, after Dodsley himself had corrected the proofs. ('Nurse Dodsley has given it a pinch or two in the cradle, that I doubt it will bear the marks as long as it lives.') In fact this 'modest, sensible and humane' man, as Isaac Reed, a Shakespearean scholar called him, had a tremendous influence on eighteenth-century literature. Indeed one of his last publishing ventures still appears each year. This is *The Annual Register*, which first appeared, edited by Edmund Burke, in 1759, five years before Dodsley's death.

Mansfield also has its place in railway pre-history. In 1819 it became one terminus of the double-track iron railway to Pinxton, eight miles away on the Cromford Canal. Bullocks, soon superseded by horses, drew the wagons up the hills. They were then uncoupled and gravity took the wagons down the other side of the inclines. Coal was the chief freight, and its price dropped by about 30% in Mansfield when the line opened, but Mansfield stone for Barry's Houses of Parliament was carried along the line to the canal in 1833. A year earlier a passenger service had been introduced on Thursdays only for the benefit of shoppers at Mansfield market. It was an extension of

19. (opposite, above) *Blyth Priory Church*

20. (below) *All Saints Church, West Markham*

this Mansfield-Pinxton line that the local coal-owners had in mind when they met at Eastwood in 1832.

The district immediately around Mansfield is largely industrial, but places like Mansfield Woodhouse and Kirkby-in-Ashfield have managed to retain some attractive areas, simply because nineteenth-century industry settled some distance away from the old village centres. Kirkby, in fact, is really a collection of separate settlements. Older residents still refer to East Kirkby as 'The Folly' because an over-enterprising developer in 1803 began to build an inn at a deserted cross roads ready to serve the boom town that he fancied would spring up there. The project was abandoned, but the developer was right except in his timing. The boom town arrived a little later, leaving the west side of the place relatively untouched today. It still has some good old buildings, including a fine Georgian rectory.

The Kirkby area has a tradition for rearing fine cricketers. Visiting a Kirkby school once, I asked a boy his name. 'Staples', he said. Yes, he was related to the two Nottinghamshire cricketers of that name. The next boy told me his name was Voce. 'You', I said to his neighbour, 'must be Larwood.' 'No, sir', he replied, 'he's in the next room.' And he was.

It used to be said that when Nottinghamshire were short of players, especially fast bowlers, they shouted down one of the pits in this area and a budding Larwood or Voce would come up. Nowadays the supply seems to be drying up, either because modern mining no longer puts strength into the shoulder and thigh muscles, or, much more likely, cricketers' earnings, except for the fortunate few in the first flight, have not risen as rapidly as those for industrial workers. It now seems easier when there is a player shortage to send a cable overseas.

North of Kirkby, on the Derbyshire border, Teversal is another charming rural oasis with a fine church that has an interesting Norman south doorway with a series of 19 medallions carved with a variety of such allegorical symbols and patterns as crosses, a holy lamb, a dove, a serpent, a priest and three fishes. But what chiefly makes Teversal 'one of the most rewarding village churches in the county', to quote Pevsner once more, is the completeness of its seventeenth-century furnishings. There is a squire's pew, lacking a fireplace but making up for it with a panelled canopy resting on four

21. (opposite) *Sir Robert Smirke's Classical Church at Markham Clinton, built for the fourth Duke of Newcastle to house his wife's tomb and to replace West Markham Church*

spiral columns, and window openings through which generations of the Molyneux family of Teversal Hall could look out over their tenants in their box pews to the elaborate family monuments on the chancel walls.

Teversal is one bright spot in a rather dreary area. Eastward of Mansfield the horizons widen, the air clears and the landscape becomes well wooded, though chiefly by conifers. Yet industry is not far way. Rainworth is a colliery village, thought its stream, Rainworth Water, has its pretty stretches, and Blidworth is two-faced. A large, dull, twentieth-century colliery village gives way, as you approach from the north, to a charming old hill-top village whose fifteenth-century church tower looks out across the Forest to the spire of Newark and even, on a very clear day, I am told, to Lincoln's towers. Blidworth is an ancient settlement. There are the remains of a presumably Iron Age fortress a mile or so to the north west and a few barrows that are even earlier. Some of the cottages that snuggle round the church have stood for three or four centuries, longer in fact than the church itself, which, apart from the tower, dates only from 1739 and contains a pulpit and some panelling from Southwell Minster, though some fragments of the old church have been re-erected in the churchyard.

It must have been in that medieval church that the ancient Rocking ceremony was first carried out. Though it lapsed two centuries before the new church was built, it was revived in 1922, and takes place annually on the Sunday nearest to the Feast of the Purification of the Blessed Virgin Mary (2 February). It represents the presentation of the Infant Christ in the Temple. What happens is that the last male child to be baptised in Blidworth is presented by the parents to the clergyman, who places the child in a beflowered wooden cradle in front of the altar. The child is then gently rocked about a dozen times during a brief service in which the child is re-dedicated in the Christian faith before he is handed back to the parents.

Blidworth is in the heart of Robin Hood country. Maid Marian is said to have lived there until she became the bride of Robin Hood; Will Scarlet is reputedly buried in the churchyard and the hated King John had a hunting lodge in Blidworth Dale. Just to the north-west is Fountain Dale, where Friar Tuck had a cell close to the source of Rainworth Water. It was there that Friar Tuck first met and fought

Robin Hood, and the moat into which Robin fell is still there, as is the well which the sober Ordnance Survey accepts as Friar Tuck's Well, but there is no trace now of the cell.

From Blidworth several pleasant roads through the coniferous woods lead to the A614 and back into Nottingham, or, as frequent road signs pronounce with a touch of the romantic, to The North. The A614 is the finest approach to the Forest and scenically the most attractive of all the trunk roads that pass through Nottinghamshire. Bisecting the county from the northern outskirts of Nottingham to the Yorkshire border at Bawtry, it parts company with the A60 at the north end of Arnold, swings north-eastward to swoop up the A6079 from Leicester and then heads northward along the eastern fringe of the Dukeries. It is still sometimes called the Old North Road, a name that derives from the days when the Great North Road split into two portions south of the county and joined up again near Blyth.

The Nottingham conurbation stops abruptly at Arnold, another of those Forest villages that grew in the early nineteenth century into a manufacturing town with the rise of the lace and hosiery trades. It is still basically, though not exclusively, a hosiery centre, and it still retains its own identity, though in the eyes of a stranger it appears to be a Nottingham suburb. Its ancient parish church of St Mary had to be closed in 1958 while the National Coal Board worked a seam immediately below. After the removal of the coal, the church was underpinned with a concrete raft, re-roofed, restored and re-consecrated in 1959.

Nearby is 79 High Street, a Georgian house—now the headquarters of Arnold Labour Party—in which Richard Parkes Bonington was born on 25 October 1802. The son of a moderately successful portrait painter who also kept a print shop in Park Row, Nottingham, before becoming keeper of the county gaol, young Bonington was an infant prodigy who was an accomplished painter by the time he was ten. When the family removed hurriedly to Calais, for the usual reasons of avoiding financial embarrassment in England, Richard became a pupil of Louis Francia, a specialist in watercolour landscapes, and developed rapidly in this medium, though he also produced many costume portraits in oils under the influence of the Venetians. In Venice in 1826 he contracted tuberculosis and he died in London two years later when he was still only 26, and at a time when his paintings were fetching as much as 3,000 guineas. 'Can you get me a print or two of Bonington's to convince you that I won't overlook him . . ?' wrote Constable to a friend on hearing of Bonington's death. Arnold certainly has rightly not overlooked this young man whose work belongs to Constable's *genre*; there is a Bonington Drive and a Bonington School, as well as the birthplace.

But the most interesting house in the Arnold district is the red brick seventeenth-century farmhouse called The Guide House, where travellers used to stop to collect a guide to see them through the Forest in much the same way that a ship now stops to pick up a pilot to see it safely past the Goodwin Sands, and for much the same reason.

Just beyond the Guide House, at the point where the A614 leaves the Mansfield road you can hardly avoid noticing a red brick tower rising like some Eastern minaret above the trees to the west, and it is worth a half mile detour along the A60 to observe this building more closely. The tower belongs to the Bestwood pumping station, built in the 1870s in the remarkably ornate style favoured by an equally remarkable Nottingham water engineer named Thomas Hawksley, who seems to have set a pattern for waterworks architecture in the East Midlands. Unfortunately Bestwood has lost its beam engines, but a few miles along the A60 at Papplewick a recently formed trust is preserving another fine pair. Whatever one may think of his taste in architecture, one must at least admire the concept of placing an ornamental garden in front of an industrial plant in rural surroundings. Hawksley was as far ahead of his time in thinking of the environment as he was in his ideas of waterworks engineering, in which Nottingham itself was then far ahead of the rest of the country.

Back on the A614 one should resist the urge to drive straight on to the Dukeries. The first road off on the right beyond the junction with the A60 leads to Calverton, which should not be missed because it is a splendid example of how agriculture and industry, the old and the new, can live harmoniously together. Like Blidworth, it is a marriage between an old Forest settlement and a modern colliery village, but here the marriage seems to have been entirely happy. This may be partly due to Calverton Colliery being slightly newer than the one at Blidworth; so that there was time to profit from experience; partly perhaps to a long 'engagement', a transition period when the village became a centre of light industry, a centre in fact of stocking making. What is certain is that the Rev William Lee and G. A. Jellicoe, three and a half centuries apart, between them saved Calverton, and the foundations have been wisely built on by more modern planners.

William Lee was a curate of Calverton who in 1589 invented the stocking frame that removed the necessity of knitting by hand. His invention was the product of frustrated love, according to the local story which is too good to question. The local girl he wanted to marry played hard to get. 'Whenever he paid his visits she always took care to be busily employed in knitting, and would pay no attention to his addresses', wrote Gravner Henson, an early nineteenth-century historian of the industry, 'and he vowed to devote his future leisure, instead of dancing attendance on a capricious woman . . . to devising an invention that should effectually supersede her favourite employment of knitting. He succeeded, and in vain did she (afterwards) try to reclaim his attention.'

The machine was an intensely complicated affair, the direct ancestor of all hosiery and lace machines. It could produce work of the highest quality at the rate of between 1,000 and 1,500 loops a minute compared with the 100 loops that was reckoned possible by hand knitting. The economic consequences were perhaps too great to be faced either by Queen Elizabeth 1 or James 1, neither of whom would grant Lee a patent or any financial aid. So Lee, with his brother James, and some local workmen cleared off to France, where Henry of Navarre was more forthcoming. But that source of income ended with Henry's assassination in 1610, and Lee died later in the same year still a poor man. James returned to Nottinghamshire, and Calverton became a local centre of the framework knitting industry. So it remained for nearly three centuries. In the middle of the nineteenth century 409 stocking frames were working in a village of some 1300 inhabitants, and some continued to work into the 1920s. Many of the stockingers' cottages survive, easily recognizable by their wide windows, and there are more modern hosiery factories at work in the village.

On to this long street village where farming and hosiery had mixed happily for so long was grafted in 1937 a large housing estate to accommodate the miners in the new Calverton Colliery. Fortunately the grafting was extremely well done by G. A. Jellicoe, who designed both the pit and the houses. Collieries can never be beautiful, but this one at least looks civilised. And the colliery houses are good by any standards.

Calverton, it seems to me, should be a good place to live in. Attractive, despite its straggle, it has all the amenities of a modern small town, including an excellent small covered shopping centre with clinic, county library and ample parking space, work enough for a population of just under 7,000, and the atmosphere of a charming village. People who stick to the old adage about 'where there's muck there's money' should look at Calverton, which seems to have prosperity without pollution.

Woodborough, a mile away, is a smaller edition of Calverton, straggling, attractive, containing a similar proportion of stockingers' cottages and a more interesting church with a fine, lofty chancel built about 1356 by Richard de Strelley, whose family held the manor for two centuries until the reign of Elizabeth 1. The road between the two villages climbs to about 300 feet near the oval hill fortress at Foxwood but the wide views make it seem much higher. It is a view that looks out towards the Trent Valley. There are orchards, parkland; it is a view that owes much to eighteenth-century landowners. Here, one is on the Keuper Marl, on the very fringe of the Forest, Eastward, a quiet lane leads back over Dorket Head, which at 484 feet is high for Nottinghamshire, to the A614. Or you can turn southwards and go back into Nottingham over Mapperley Plains, which are heavily built over, but still offer wide views across the Trent Valley.

CHAPTER FIVE

The Dukeries

Sherwood Forest, for most people, means the Dukeries. Within this roughly pear-shaped area about ten miles long from Worksop in the north to Rufford in the south and eight miles across at its widest, is a tract of undulating country—mostly below the 300 ft contour line—containing a fascinating patchwork of mixed farms, parkland and forest. But it is the forest that stirs the imagination. Among the ancient oaks in the old King's Hays of Birklands and Bilhaugh it becomes harder to dismiss Robin Hood and his merry men as mere figures in popular mythology. Wandering alone along the forest paths you can easily imagine figures in Lincoln green lurking in the cover of substantial oaks.

In medieval times this area of Sherwood was as inhospitable to man through its light sandy soils and dense coverings of woodland and undergrowth as through its savage forest laws. The first large-scale attempt to tame this wilderness began with the coming of the Cistercians to Rufford in 1148 and the arrival of the Premonstratensians at Welbeck five years later. They enclosed some land for their sheep whose wool was dispatched to the Flemish and Italian markets. After the Dissolution 'the silent nibbling of the Forest by the monastic sheep and oxen was succeeded by the bustling enterprise of their lay successors', as J. D. Chambers put it in his *Nottinghamshire in the Eighteenth Century*. Over the next two centuries green parkland replaced black heath and tangled undergrowth, and great mansions sprang up out of the innumerable rabbit warrens.

Above all the new sounds that echoed down the once silent forest glades in these bustling centuries the ring of the woodsman's axe rose most sharply as ancient oaks and birches crashed. What began as controlled clearance by the new landowners gave way to the more urgent needs of the navy in the Civil War and afterwards, as well as the demands of iron and lead smelters. By 1641 there was 'not so much as a Bush for a Nightingale to rest in . . .', according to an anonymous writer of the time, and 14 years later the verderers reported 'the Forest is ruined'. In 1670 there was said to be 'not any more timber left in the forest', hardly surprising perhaps if a Mr Clark, who in Commonwealth times had 'received a grant for the sale of traitors' estates', carried out his plan to take 28,000 trees.

There may have been an element of exaggeration in these agonised cries, but even so Defoe, in his *Tour of England and Wales* in 1724 was able to write 'this forest does not add to the fruitfulness of the county, for 'tis now, as it were, given up to waste: even the woods which formerly made it so famous for thieves, are wasted; and if there was such a man as Robin Hood . . . he could hardly find shelter for one, if he was now to have been there'.

But the picture was soon to change. The holocaust was followed by a century of intensive private enclosing and planting, often at the expense of the villagers' common rights and of the Crown, whose property was gradually whittled away until, in 1806, it disposed of its last holdings—Birklands—to the Duke of Portland. The 1778 edition of Defoe's *Tour* was able to report that 'the Dukes of Norfolk, Kingston, Newcastle and Portland have made prodigious plantations. Sir George Saville has planted a whole country: so the Sherwood Forest may once again be clothed in all the dignity of wood.'

That the Dukeries are so clothed today is due in part to these noble landowners and their successors. Even in the second half of the nineteenth century, when tree planting had become less fashionable, Sherwood was one of the few areas in the country where the woodland area increased.

Then came two wars, and, inevitably, more felling. Fortunately, between the two wars (in 1919) the Forestry Commission was formed, and soon began planting in Sherwood, specially in the Dukeries. These plantations, not old enough then to provide wartime timber, have been doubled since 1945. Today the Forestry Commission holds more than 15,000 acres in Sherwood of which over 14,000 acres have been planted. New planting is going on equally rapidly in more than 8,000 acres of private woodland, keeping pace with the best late-eighteenth century rate and more than replacing wartime fellings.

But the appearance of the Dukeries is changing. Whereas the

eighteenth-century landowners planted oaks, beech, sweet chestnut and sycamore, with some pines and larches, the emphasis has altered. Today 70% of the plantings are pines—mostly Corsican pine, with some Scots pine and a few Japanese larch and other conifers—and only 15% hardwood, mainly beech.

This policy is not generally popular. Pinewoods are sombre and lack the beauty of the traditional British deciduous forests. The Forestry Commission has come in for some harsh criticism, not all of it fair. Its policy is forced upon it by economic necessity. Softwood is in greater demand than hardwood and more profitable; it is better suited to the light, sandy soils of Sherwood, and stands up better—the Corsican pines in particular—to air pollution from industry. And it must be said that the change is not always immediately apparent. The Commission, with a sidelong glance at its critics, plants belts of birch alongside roads and tracks. It has also left intact, and in some cases helped to protect, the ancient oaks that have survived from the days when the Dukeries were part of a royal forest.

There is something to be said for approaching the Dukeries from the south-west along the Ollerton road from Mansfield in order to see another reminder of those days. This is a fragment of a medieval stone wall, marked on the map as King John's Palace. It was in fact a hunting lodge built before John's reign to give royalty a closer access to the Forest than was offered by the Manor House of Mansfield. Henry I enclosed it in a park in 1180 and Edward III enlarged it. In between, the two earlier Edwards used it frequently and tradition says that it was the meeting place of Richard I and Robin Hood. It was abandoned at the end of the fifteenth century and is today a sad sight, less impressive than either the pair of tall headstocks, appropriately painted Lincoln green, of Clipstone Colliery, or Archway Lodge, a mile or so to the north. This latter building is a splendidly preserved stone archway with living accommodation on either side, a school-room above, and figures of Robin Hood, Maid Marion, Friar Tuck, Little John, Allan-a-Dale and Richard I set in niches in the walls. Built by the fourth Duke of Portland between 1842 and 1844, it bestrides a ride which reputedly was intended to extend from Welbeck Abbey into Nottingham. If this sounds improbable it is no more improbable than the irrigation canal north of Clipstone called the Flood Dike on which he spent £80,000 in converting a soggy valley into excellent pasture.

On the whole, though, the best way to reach the Dukeries from the south is the traditional route along the A614. Along this road you have attractive scenery all the way from Nottingham, except for a short stretch where there is an unfortunate view of the colliery village of Bilsthorpe too prominent on a hillside to the east. But whichever way you choose, Rufford Abbey should be your first call.

Strictly speaking, Rufford does not belong to the Dukeries at all as its owners never broke the marquisate barrier, and with four Dukes around this cut little ice. The official boundary of the Dukeries is the River Maun, a mile to the north, but only the severest pedant would exclude Rufford, the ford on Rainworth Water where the Cistercians founded their only Nottinghamshire abbey. There they lived quietly for nearly four centuries, entertained Edward 1 and Queen Eleanor in 1290, felled and sold timber, grazed their sheep and sold the wool, and allegedly committed the unmentionable misdemeanours which Commissioners Legh and Layton made a point of mentioning as an excuse for suppression, along with most of the other smaller houses, in 1536.

Of the medieval abbey, or its three water mills, nothing remains except a vaulted crypt with round pillars. Indeed, little remained by the end of the sixteenth century because as Henry viii granted the estate to George, Earl of Shrewsbury, it soon passed into the hands of his daughter-in-law, Bess of Hardwick, who with her usual energy, rebuilt the house to suit her own taste. Further alterations and additions were made by the Savile family over the next two centuries, but most of these have gone too. After being occupied by the army during the last war, and unoccupied afterwards, most of it was demolished when it was considered unsafe in the 1950s. The remains are being gradually restored by the Department of the Environment and are not generally accessible to the public. 'Very melancholy', the expression used by the Honourable John Byng (later Lord Torrington) on a visit to Rufford in 1789, would today be an equally apt comment for the house in which Bess pulled off her most daring coup.

This was the marriage of her daughter, Elizabeth Cavendish, to Charles Stuart, Earl of Lennox, brother of Darnley, Mary, Queen of Scots' husband. Through his mother, Lennox was third in the line of succession for the throne, so Bess was clearly aiming high when she travelled to Huntingdon in the autumn of 1574, intercepted the Countess of Lennox and her son on a return journey from London to Scotland, and persuaded them to stay with her at Rufford. In the private chapel there the couple were married after a whirlwind courtship of five days. Queen Elizabeth I was not amused by the marriage, as she made clear in a letter to the Earl of Shrewsbury, who rather ungallantly attributed all the blame to his wife. The Queen was even less amused when the marriage was blessed with a daughter, Lady Arbella Stuart. The story from then on, beginning with the death of Elizabeth Lennox in childbirth, is pure tragedy, but as it was not played out in Nottinghamshire it would be inappropriate to deal with it here.

Let us then return to Rufford for a brief mention of the Savile family, who inherited by marriage. The most famous of them was that remarkable seventeenth-century figure Sir George Savile, who in fairly rapid succession was created a baron, a viscount and finally Marquis of Halifax, but is better remembered as 'The Trimmer', because of a political opportunism worthy of Bess herself. He made some additions to Rufford, but was accused by his son of neglecting the estate, which he rarely visited as he became more politically involved. This could not be said of an eighteenth-century successor, Sir George Savile, who sat in the Commons through five successive Parliaments but still found time to plant more than 1,000 acres at Rufford with oak and ash. It was not before time, apparently, for five years after Sir George's death Byng reported 'there are few trees of much size', adding that there was 'gloom without grandeur, and shade without timber'.

That could hardly be said today. The grounds became a country park in 1970 and are always open to the public. The County Council has spent more than £15,000 to restore the lake, 'ditch-like' in Byng's time, which you can now fish for a fairly nominal daily charge, and is now spending a further £20,000 over two years to improve certain other areas in the park, which has lost its gloom and is now recovering its grandeur.

Almost opposite the main entrance to Rufford is a former lodge or toll house now a restaurant serving, among other meals, admirable afternoon teas. This fact is worth recording because afternoon teas are not easy to find in Nottinghamshire, although there are numerous places where one can obtain excellent lunches or evening meals at prices which are usually good value but not the sort of thing that most of us can afford every day without benefit of expense account. That they are usually fullish must reflect the general prosperity of the area. And, as a sandwich and half-pint lunch man myself, I must say that most of these places met my simple needs without any obvious raising of eyebrows. It is a lot easier to get some sort of meal on the spur of the moment in Britain today than it was before the war—except at tea-time.

Behind this isolated restaurant, and stretching away to the south-west to occupy almost all the land between the A611 and the A614 are the 4,000 acres of Rufford and Clipstone Forests. This land was mostly felled woodland (a First World War casualty), heath and derelict pasture when the Forestry Commission negotiated a 999 years lease with the Rufford and Welbeck estates and started planting in 1925. It was the Commission's first large scale planting in Sherwood. The thinning of these and other young plantations in the forest began after the last war and now yields close on 20,000 tons of timber a year, much of it from Rufford and Clipstone. If this sounds like a reversion to the seventeenth-century denudation of the Forest, I should add that 100 acres are replanted annually along with a further 40 acres of fresh planting.

Two miles north of Rufford, Ollerton cross-roads offer a bewildering choice of routes, all of which have their attractions. From here it is possible to make a circular tour of the Dukeries, but it is worth a short diversion to look at the charming centre of Ollerton village. It has one of the finest war memorials I have seen, a garden of shrubs on a small island by a working water mill. Close by is the Hop Pole Inn, 'pleasantly situated on a trout stream, and fronting the forest woods', according to Byng, who found it 'a house of good stop and station'. It is a solid looking Georgian coaching inn, and its sign is a reminder that hop growing flourished in the area until well into the last century. New Ollerton is a bustling colliery village that sprang up with the sinking of a new mine in 1925, but has little visual attraction.

The same could almost be said of Edwinstowe, on the west side of the cross-roads. The biggest village in the Dukeries, with a population of 4,000 likely to double in the near future, it is a dreary mining village dominated by its colliery—until you find Church Street. Here, church and hall, with a few other pleasant houses carry you back to the late eighteenth century when a contemporary local historian thought 'the village may be considered one of the decent sort'. It certainly has a long history. Tradition says its name derives from the temporary burial there of King Edwin after he was killed by Penda, King of Mercia, at the battle of Hatfield in 633. An even stronger tradition makes the church the scene of the wedding of Robin Hood and Maid Marion. Even for those disinclined to respect tradition it is an interesting church with a prominent spire and a Norman door on the south side of the chancel. It dates essentially from the twelfth and thirteenth centuries, though it has been restored often since then, notably in 1672 when the people of Edwinstowe petitioned to buy 200 decayed oaks from Birklands and Bilhaugh to repair their 'ruinous church'.

Just past the church the Forest starts. It is most unexpected. Church Street ends in a large clearing; there is a delightful cricket ground; often in summer an old-fashioned fair; beyond are the trees of Birklands, oaks and silver birch mostly, the latter accounting for the name. But it is the oaks that claim your attention most. Their ages vary widely. Some may be as much as 600 years old and were standing when the courts of attachment were held at Edwinstowe every six weeks. They were among the 21,000 oaks that were counted in Birklands in 1609.

The most famous of these is the Major Oak, so named not, as you might imagine, for its pre-eminence but, it is said, in honour of Major Rooke the local historian. Before the nineteenth century it was called the Queen Oak. Estimates of its age vary between a highly improbable 1500 years and a conservative 500, but there is general acceptance of a 30-ft girth and 270-ft as the circumference of its branches. Twelve people can stand fairly comfortably inside the hollow trunk in which Robin Hood reputedly hid. The tree lost its crown in a storm, and the feet of the 200,000 visitors who walk round it each summer have added to the damage done by age and weather. In 1972 the County Council paid around £400 to a team of tree surgeons to hack out dead wood, fill in cavities and put in extra steel cables to hold up sagging boughs.

The Major Oak stands on a well-defined track which forms part of a most interesting nature trail in summer and is inside what is now the Sherwood Country Park. This may sound tame but in fact you can be alarmingly lost if you take the wrong track or stray off into the dense bracken that carpets much of Birklands. You need not be hyper-sensitive to atmosphere to feel a sense of panic at being alone among the malformed trees that seem to belong to some primeval forest. Even from the safety of a car on the road that skirts Birklands, you may sense something almost evil in these dead misshapen trees. 'In Birkland', it was recorded in 1794, 'there was an open wood of large oak, but mostly decayed and stagheaded', the oaks having been pollarded at some time, with decay setting in from the top downwards, and you feel that these must be those same trees.

All this may seem fanciful, but there is another, very real, fear that grips the foresters, particularly in summer. This is the fear of fire. Five tall towers at different points in the Forest are lookout posts from which early warning of fires can be given, and all too often even an early warning can be too late to prevent serious damage. There has been nothing in recent times to equal the great fire of 1624 that devastated an area of woodland four miles long and half a mile wide, but an unpleasant outbreak that ignited ammunition still lying around after wartime military occupation cleared a square mile of Clumber Park in 1947, and on a single day in a recent summer 128 fires broke out in different parts of the Dukeries.

The fire risk comes from different quarters, not least from 'controlled' burning of stubble. The biggest menace, however, in an area that attracts visitors from a radius of 60 miles or more, is the public, especially from what one forester described as 'the lesser solitary picnicker', the man who wants to get away from the crowd and forgets to stub out his cigarette before leaving his secluded retreat.

Other hazards confront the foresters. They can do little about gales, such as those recorded in 1222 and 1714, or the one they vividly recall that destroyed 30,000 cubic feet of timber in the Dukeries in February 1962. But they can and do wage war against those other menaces: the rabbit, the grey squirrel and the hare, in that order of magnitude. The young oak saplings in Birklands and Bilhaugh mostly date from the years immediately after the myxomatosis epidemic in the 1950s. Very young saplings are unlikely to have survived the renewal of grazing now that rabbits are back to something like 80% of their pre-epidemic numbers in the Dukeries (though less numerous in the southern part of the Forest).

There are still deer in Sherwood, fallow mostly, with some red and perhaps an occasional roe, but their total number probably does not exceed 200 and is controlled by a trained stalker who culls about ten a year of the weakest specimens, leaving the strong to breed. They are rarely seen by visitors, except in Thoresby Park, but in winter they sometimes visit gardens and fields on the edge of the Forest to feed on brussels sprouts and other vegetables, though without causing anything like the problems that followed the seventeenth-century timber clearance. Constantly disturbed by felling at that time, they sought food and shelter on the forest fringes, enraging landowners and tenants, who complained bitterly in 1708 of 'the grievous and almost intolerable burden we labour under by reason of the numerous increase of the red deer', estimated at 900 head. This burden was lifted by the united efforts of keepers and farmers. Defoe reported in 1724 the absence of 'any store of deer, compared to the quantity which in former times they tell us there usually was'. By 1793 they had been almost exterminated, making unnecessary the guarding of wheatfields 'by horns by day and by fire at night'. Larger herds continued to graze in the parks at Thoresby and Welbeck until 1939 when the red deer at Welbeck and the fallow at Thoresby had to be drastically reduced. Most of the red left in the Dukeries are descendants from survivors of the Welbeck herd.

The eighteenth-century reduction of the deer population, followed almost immediately by the introduction locally of the swede turnip, brought striking agricultural improvements to an area that Arthur Young considered 'highly improvable', but even more rapid improvements have been made since the last war. New fertilisers, reducing the emphasis on sheep-rearing for manuring purposes, have added greater fertility to the light, ill-drained land, resulting in increased attention to milk-production. The 'ill-managed farms' of Young's day have been replaced by efficient mixed farms. Large areas of wasteland have gone over to arable and to the production of sugar beet. At Thoresby, for instance, a 1,500-acre home farm has been carved out of parklands and roughlands since the last war.

Thoresby is the southernmost of the ducal estates which form one great wedge of land between Ollerton and Worksop. It is the only house occupied by descendants of its original owners and the only one open to the public. Lying within the triangle formed by the

A614 and A6009, it can be approached almost equally attractively along either road from Ollerton cross-roads, though the latter road has the advantage of passing through Bilhaugh, which, like Birklands, still has survivors from the 28,900 oaks that stood there in 1609.

It was out of Bilhaugh that Robert Pierrepont, first Earl of Kingston, a son-in-law of Bess of Hardwick carved the great park, now 3,000 acres in extent, to surround the estate he had acquired in 1633. There had been a house at Thoresby as early as Elizabeth I's reign, which might have been replaced sooner if the Civil War had not intervened, splitting the family evenly, with the Earl sitting astride the fence and his two sons on either side. So it was left to William, the fourth Earl, to instruct William Talman, subsequently architect of Chatsworth, to build the first Pierrepont house. This was destroyed by fire in 1745, and was succeeded by 'a comfortable house' designed by John Carr of York for the fourth Earl's successor who had been created Duke of Kingston-upon-Hull for his loyalty in the '15 rebellion. He was the father of the redoubtable Lady Mary Wortley Montagu, traveller, wit, blue-stocking and pioneer of inoculation against small-pox, who spent much of her early life at Thoresby before rejecting the bridegroom her father had nominated and forcing the cold, pompous Edward Wortley to elope with her in a romantic manner that was quite outside his normal formal style. This startling event led to separation from her father and Thoresby—and eventually from Mr Wortley—but not immediately from Nottinghamshire, as she stayed often at Wallingwells, 11 miles from Thoresby, in the early years of her marriage.

Later in the eighteenth century Thoresby was to be owned by a woman even more remarkable, in a different way, than Lady Mary. This was 'the Duchess Robin Hood', as Horace Walpole called her. She was born Elizabeth Chudleigh, became a maid of honour—an ironic title—to Augusta, Princess of Wales, and in 1744, when she was 20, secretly married a young naval officer, Lieutenant Augustus Hervey. They lived together briefly when his naval duties permitted, but separated in 1747 and never met again. Two years later she became mistress of the second Duke of Kingston, 'a very weak man of the greatest beauty and the finest person in England', according to Walpole. Hankering after becoming the legal Duchess, she wrote to Hervey in 1768 suggesting a divorce. He was at first willing, but

22. (opposite) *Open field system at Laxton, with Laxton Church on the ridge in background*

ROBERT DENISON, Esq.
Died 20ᵗʰ March 1785, Aged 65.

changed his mind on discovering that he would become responsible for her debts amounting to £16,000. She then brought an action before the Ecclesiastical Court, which surprisingly pronounced her 'a spinster', a title which she promptly changed to become Duchess of Kingston in a ceremony at St George's, Hanover Square. Five years later the Duke died, after considerately disinheriting his nephew and leaving her his entire fortune. This led to the public washing of much dirty linen and to the appearance of the Duchess at Westminster in 1775 to face a charge of bigamy. She was found guilty, but on account of her rank she was discharged on payment of fees. After a stay at St Petersburg with her friend the Empress Catherine, she returned to England to die in 1788 at the age of 63, easing her way into the next world by taking two glasses of Madeira before expiring.

When Byng visited Thoresby the following year 'the foolish expence and vanity of this duchess' was visible in every room, and 'all the gaudy furniture and useless china' was about to be sold. It was 'neither a pretty place, or of taste, or comfort', nor was it a ducal house, the title having died with the second Duke. But the Pierreponts continued to live there, and a nephew of the second Duke became Earl Manvers in 1806. His grandson, the third Earl, found Carr's Georgian house too cramped for comfort and in 1864 called in Anthony Salvin, fresh from restoring Windsor Castle, to build him something more spacious.

Salvin did just that. The present Thoresby is reputedly the largest Victorian house in England. It took eleven years to complete. Pevsner describes it as 'far more ambitious than any other of the Victorian age in the country, and a lasting monument to the self-confidence of at least one section of the nineteenth century nobility'. It is a splendid exercise in neo-Tudor exuberance, a sort of latter-day Wollaton, with a central tower in the Burghley style above the entrance on the east front. The statistics of the place are bewildering. The east front is 182-ft long, almost the length of three cricket pitches. The south front is a mere two feet shorter. The great hall, running through three storeys is 65-ft by 31-ft, and has a bay window 24-ft high. Nobody seems quite to know how many rooms there are; there are 29 on the *piano nobile* alone.

But there is more to Thoresby than size. Its great hall, with a fine hammer-beam roof, is superb; so is the blue drawing room and its plaster ceiling based on the Salons of the French Rococo period. I

23. (opposite) *Monument by Nollekens to Robert Denison in Ossington Church*

can gaze for hours at the elaborately carved fireplace in the library with statues in wood of Robin Hood and Little John, the work of a Mansfield carver who spent three rewarding years on the carving. There is, too, a splendid statue of Robin Hood in the centre of the courtyard, executed by Tussaud-Birt, a grandson of Mme Tussaud, and reached through a fine pair of wrought iron gates. There are other treasures, including a collection of elegant clocks, but to me the most significant thing about Thoresby is historical. It is the last of the great stately homes, marking the end of a chapter in our social history; and it signs off with a proud, defiant flourish.

At each end of Thoresby's 65-acre lake, formed by damming the River Meden, is a village; Budby on the west, Perlethorpe on the east. They sound like Danish settlements, look like fairly modern estate villages and are in fact both. Budby is a modest model village of simple cottages with Gothic windows strung out along the main Ollerton-Worksop road as it forms a gentle S-bend; a piece of early ribbon building by the first Earl Manvers in 1807. At each end of the village is a large farm, and on a grassy slope to the east is Budby Castle (or William's Castle), a battlemented Gothic folly-house. Perlethorpe's cottages are older but undistinguished, though quite attractively set around a green near to the Meden, and the Home Farm is delightful. So is the parish church, built by Salvin in the Decorated style in 1876. It should not be missed, but often is, largely because the Duke of Newcastle trumped Earl Manvers' ace by building an even more elaborate church ten years later at Clumber.

The Clumber estate adjoins Thoresby. It lies in the valley of the River Poulter, the northernmost of the three rivers that cut through the Bunter sandstone. There is no mansion to see, the Duke having demolished it in 1938, eight years before selling the 4,000 acre park to the National Trust, who were financially supported in the purchase by a consortium of eight local authorities. But this does not deter visitors. Nearly a million of them pass through one or other of the five impressive park gates annually. Most of them come by car; in about 5,000 cars on a typical summer Sunday, and they leave behind enough litter to occupy six assistant wardens for two whole days, three after a Bank Holiday.

If this makes Clumber sound a crowded, messy place, the impression is false. Only the area around the main car park in front of the lake ever appears crowded and the mess is only evident when the cars move off. Away from this small area you can get all the seclusion and freedom you want in enchanting surroundings that bear no resemblance to the 'black heath, full of rabbits, having a narrow river running through it with a small boggy close or two' that was there little more than two centuries ago, though in fact it still has the largest area of heathland in Sherwood—over 600 acres—today one of Clumber's main attractions.

Of all the Dukeries' great estates it is the most recent creation and the largest, being over ten miles in circumference, but as a settlement it was occupied before 1086 and had grown into a hamlet by the mid-sixteenth century. Then in 1707 the Duke of Newcastle wrote to Queen Anne suggesting that a park might be made of at least 3,000 acres '. . . for the better improvement and ornament of her Majestyes Forest of Sherwood . . . and for ye ease of ye proprietors and tennants of lands adjoining to that part of the said forest . . .' And no doubt for his own ease too, though it is only fair to say that not until 1770 was a mansion built on the site.

That was built for the first Pelham-Clinton Duke of Newcastle, which is the cue for an attempt to explain the absurdly complicated dukedom. The main complication lies in the fact that the title was thrice created. The first Duke of Newcastle-on-Tyne was a Cavendish, son, it is almost superfluous to say, of Bess of Hardwick. Welbeck was his Nottinghamshire seat. The title died with the second Duke, but was re-created for his son-in-law, John Hollies, fourth Earl of Clare. While he lived, Clumber and Welbeck were united for the only time. On his death Clumber passed to a nephew who became Duke of Newcastle of the third creation, a title which would have died out in 1768 if the last of that line had not been given a second Dukedom, that of Newcastle-under-Lyme, which is the one that continues today. The family name became Pelham-Hollies-Fiennes-Clinton, which they sensibly shortened to Pelham-Clinton.

The architect of Clumber was Stephen Wright, not one of the best known names in an age of fine architects, but he did well enough there to evoke from Byng the comment, 'I think it is the best house I ever enter'd.' It was a remarkable tribute from one who detested new houses. Wright's house was never superseded but it was damaged by several fires and enlarged twice, first by Sir Charles Barry, architect of the Houses of Parliament, in 1857, and then by his son, also Charles, in 1879. Only the rectangular, red brick stable block has survived, its south-west wing from the eighteenth century.

Several of Wright's buildings remain around the park. To north and south of the lake that was formed by damming the Poulter are two Doric temples, one of Roman and the other of Greek design. Even more impressive is the bridge that spans the Poulter just before it widens out to form the lake. Built of ashlar, with three almost semi-circular arches, it is a noble monument to the elegance and grace of the period, and in Byng's time it afforded the best view of the mansion.

Most of the splendid entrance gates and lodges date from the eighteenth century, and all are listed as being of architectural and historical importance. The finest of all is the Aspley Head gate, off the A614. It has an arched gateway of ashlar surmounted by the family coat of arms. Symmetrical lodges stand at either side. Beyond is the famous lime tree avenue, arguably the finest avenue of trees in England. Two miles long, it has a double row of trees on either side—1,296 trees in all.

If that sounds a lot of timber, it represents only a fraction of all the Clumber trees, which are as richly varied as they are prolific. The deciduous woodland contains a mixture of oak, beech, sweet chestnut and sycamore, with red oak prominent in more recent plantations. All these species occur again in the mixed woodland, as well as Corsican and Scots pine, European and hybrid larches. The Forestry Commission plantations around the perimeter are dominated by the pines, screened by birch and red oak to form fire breaks as well as for scenic reasons.

Wandering amongst the trees, you realise that something like a miracle has been performed at Clumber—twice. The first occurred in the eighteenth century when this estate was created out of that 'black heath' and its 'few boggy closes'. No wonder the usually astringent Byng became almost lyrical about the 'wonderful and hourly improvement', though there were setbacks. Ten years after Byng's visit 1,800 acres of land reclaimed for agriculture was allowed to revert to heathland because the poor quality of the soil defeated the improvers. But if some battles were lost, the improvers won the war against the waste. And then in 1946 a new generation had to tackle a new campaign. For seven years the estate had been occupied by the military.

There had been no maintenance, much damage. Many of the trees had been felled, others were nearing the end of their lives. The place was in a sad state when the newly created Clumber Park Management Committee set about the work of restoration. When you have seen for yourself what they have done you will probably agree that the recovery has been almost miraculous.

The revived Clumber is a superb monument to the late Mr John Trayner. As East Midland Area Agent for the National Trust, he had his office in the park, and was responsible to the Committee for its daily management from 1946 until ill-health compelled his premature retirement in 1970. His enthusiasm and imagination nursed Clumber back to life.

Some of his enthusiasm infected me when he first showed me over Clumber Church, a vast, elaborate Victorian Gothic, town church in a setting that Pevsner aptly calls 'poignantly beautiful and inappropriate', and 'an eerie memorial to the passing of an age'. Certainly there are few men today who could or would spend more than £30,000 on building a private chapel to celebrate their coming of age, as did the seventh Duke of Newcastle. Whether or not you approve of the result is a matter of individual opinion, but you can hardly fail to be impressed by your first sight of the structure of red Runcorn sandstone and white limestone from nearby Steetley, with its tall spire stretching up above the backcloth of oaks, cedars and limes from its square, buttressed central tower.

The surprising thing about the interior is the narrowness of the nave. There are no aisles, just wall passages each side over blind arcades. The lack of width is accentuated by the height of the vaulted roof, the absence of lower windows, and by the unusually large transepts. The altar, raised above the marble floor of the chancel, is bathed in light because the two flanking windows of plain glass have been deliberately carried lower than the others. The exceptionally long chancel—only slightly shorter than the nave—and the heavy oak rood screens, are typical of an age which laid great stress on the importance of the chancel and its separation from the congregation in the nave.

The architect, George Frederick Bodley, was renowned for his ornamentation, well represented here by the carvings on the white alabaster High Altar, the reredos of the Lady Chapel altar and on the ceiling over the font. Several large stone figures are his too, as is the stone pulpit, a gift from the people of Worksop. The wood carvings by the Rev Ernest Geldhart are exquisite, except perhaps the font cover with its vague suggestion of the Albert Memorial. There are fine Kempe windows, wrought ironwork by the estate blacksmiths and an organ which is unusual not only in its precarious position high up on the north wall of the chancel but also because it is blown hydraulically.

Services are held once a Sunday each summer when visitors join local worshippers, mainly from the estate village of Hardwick, originally Herthwick, or herd-farm. This was rebuilt towards the end of the eighteenth century as 'a sort of colony of workmen employed by the duke about the house and on the estate', according to a writer in 1826. It lies to the east of the lake and is reached by a drive running from the mid-nineteenth century Normanton Gate, opposite the handsome Normanton Inn on the A614, to cross the Poulter over the longest ford in the county. The Grange, the home farm, lies close by the water, with a dovecote a little to the east. On rising ground a quarter of a mile to the north stands Hardwick Terrace, a cluster of nineteenth-century brick cottages with steeply-pitched roofs and extravagantly tall chimneys. A few more cottages scattered amongst the trees complete an attractively planned village in a charming setting.

Related, but much later, steep roofs and tall chimneys recur amongst the newer development in Carburton, the village just outside the west fringe of Clumber Park. The older part of the village stands on slightly higher ground by the splendid seventeenth-century Manor Farm and tiny Norman chapel, which makes an interesting contrast with the lavishness of Clumber chapel. Carburton's parish register goes back to 1528, as does neighbouring Perlethorpe's, and there is said to be only one other in England as old, going back ten years before it became compulsory to keep official records. The village is in fact an old one that has declined in size since the closure of the iron forge that was once worked by George Sitwell of Renishaw and later by the local Spencer family. It looks today an incongruous setting for an ironworks, but in fact it had the essential requirements: water, and plentiful timber. The forge was flourishing in 1751, when 'the pigs were brought from Derbyshire to be melted into bars for use', but the only traces today are the Forge Mill Dam, west of the village, and a Charcoal Plantation.

Two miles higher up the Poulter, sandwiched between Corunna Hill and Bunker Hill, each a mere 170-ft, is Norton, an unpretentious piece of eighteenth- and nineteenth-century ribbon building along what was then a main road from Warsop through Welbeck Park but is now a quiet country lane. There is neither pub nor church, and little modern development except for a group of estate bungalows at the north end of the village.

Worshippers of God and Bacchus have to go a mile southward to Cuckney to satisfy their needs, but are rewarded by two interesting buildings close together in a noisy, yet attractive, but rather odd village. The noise comes from the heavy industrial traffic on the three main roads that cross here; the attraction from its many good buildings; the oddity from its division into two quite distinct parts: one agricultural, the other industrial, but both mainly eighteenth century in character.

It was the roads, fording the Poulter on an island in the marshy ground, that account for Cuckney's early importance and for the motte-and-bailey castle guarding the ford, and their changing pattern that explains the division of the village. Because of the boggy ground the church, with its exceptionally long twelfth-century nave, is now supported on a concrete raft to prevent subsidence. The sinking of this raft exposed the mass grave of nearly 200 men, a relic of some quite forgotten disaster. Church and castle mound nestle together to the north east of the village, with the 'Greendale Oak' on the other side of a minor road. This interesting pub takes its unusual name from a famous tree on the Welbeck estate through which a roadway was cut in 1724, enabling the first Duke of Portland to drive a coach and four through it to win a wager with the Earl of Oxford.

The Domesday Book recorded two mills at Cuckney in 1086, but it was the building of mills of a different kind that caused its late-eighteenth century expansion. 'Its present consequence', wrote a local historian of the time, 'has been occasioned by the worsted and other manufactury established lately here'. Many apprentice children, mainly aged eight to ten years, were employed, apparently in idyllic conditions. 'They live in cottages, built for the purpose, under the care of superintendents: boys under one roof and girls under another. An apothecary attends them at stated times to preserve health. They are trained to duties of religion and are fed plentifully. It is happy that these little aliens to kindred affection should, by the bounty of the good and opulent, be made useful members of society and monuments of philanthropy.' Nevertheless, more than a third of these happy monuments either died, absconded, or returned to Overseers or parents in the 20 years from 1786.

Some of these admirable industrial buildings survive, including the workers' cottages, as well as the mill-pond and the fine wrought-iron railings that enclose its outlet chamber. What is left of the mills is now the village school, replacing, it seems, a building that has been converted into a pleasant house.

Nearby is the home of Marksmen Archery Products, which claims to produce more bows and arrows than any other firm outside the U.S.A. Four fletchers make 2,000 arrows a week, and ten bowyers produce 5,000 bows a year. Some of this equipment made in the Sherwood Forest is sold abroad. The Russian archery team used £5,000 worth of bows and arrows from Cuckney at the Munich Olympic Games in 1972.

The Worksop road (A60) from Cuckney curves gracefully round the western fringe of the Welbeck Abbey estate. This is literally the only surviving Dukery, though in fact the Duke of Portland no longer lives at the Abbey but in a smaller house called Welbeck Woodhouse that was built in the grounds in 1932. The Abbey now houses Welbeck College, offering a two-year sixth-form boarding school education in preparation for cadetship at Sandhurst. It is not open to the public, though the grounds occasionally are.

Thomas de Cuckney founded the Abbey for a colony of Praemonstratensian Canons (White Canons) from Newhouse in Lincolnshire near the end of Henry II's reign, and it prospered to such an extent that in 1512 it became the parent of the seven other English houses of the order. At the Dissolution Henry VIII granted it to Richard Whalley of Shelford, but in due course it passed, like most other properties in these parts, into the capacious hands of Bess of Hardwick. She left it to her son Sir Charles Cavendish, father of the Sir William who ran up the scales of the peerage to become Earl, Marquis and Duke of Newcastle. The last title was granted by Charles II in 1664 in compensation for the loss of more than £940,000 that he suffered for his Civil War support for the Royalists.

As a soldier, Clarendon said: 'He liked the pomp and absolute authority of a general well, and preserved the dignity of it to the full . . . . But the substantial part and fatigue of a general he did not in any degree understand, being utterly unacquainted with war.' He was more accomplished in horsemanship and the arts, combining the two in a book on the art of training horses, with liberal illustrations that feature the horses less than the Duke. But his devotion to horses was genuine, though it only just exceeded his love for his second wife, Charles Lamb's 'thrice noble, chaste and virtuous, but somewhat fantistical and original brained Margaret Newcastle'.

Her copious, tedious literary work now lies embalmed in the British Museum. At Welbeck it is easier to remember the Duke's love of horses than of his wife. His riding house and stables, that Pevsner surprisingly dismisses as 'utilitarian Jacobean', are the best buildings at Welbeck and seem to me to be amongst the best in Nottinghamshire. They were built for the first Duke by Huntingdon Smythson, relative of the 'architector' of Wollaton, in 1623–25, and with the estate houses and workshops form a splendid separate settlement half a mile up the main drive from the A60 and thus reasonably accessible to the casual visitor.

Through several marriages Welbeck passed into the hands of the Bentinck family (now Cavendish-Bentinck) in the person of the second Duke of Portland. Neither he nor his successor regarded Welbeck as his principal seat, making more use of Bulstrode, near Beaconsfield, which was handier for London, an essential requirement for the third Duke, who became Prime Minister in 1782 on the death of the Marquis of Rockingham. He was very much a compromise choice, according to his grandson Charles Greville. 'My grandfather was a very honourable, high-minded but ordinary man; his abilities were very second-rate, and he had no power of speaking; and his election to the post of leader of the great Whig only shows how aristocratic that party was, and what weight and influence the aristocracy possessed in those days. . . .'

Coincidentally, the fourth Duke's son, Lord George Bentinck, also became an unwilling compromise party leader, this time of the Tory opposition. He described himself modestly as 'Virtually an uneducated man, never intended or attracted by taste for a political life, in the House of Commons only by a pure accident—indeed by an undesired and inevitable chance—I am well aware of my own incapacity properly to fill the station I have been thrust into', which is something that might have been said by many party leaders—but probably never has been. But it is as a politician of the Turf that Lord George is chiefly remembered. What was becoming the sport of crooks was transformed by this 'Lord Paramount of the Turf' into the 'sport of kings'. In the process of cleaning up racing he inevitably made enemies, and when he was found dead in Welbeck Park in 1848 there were rumours of foul play. Medical evidence did not support this theory, but the legend is still occasionally heard.

There are legends too about the fifth Duke of Portland, but the truth about this extraordinary character is too remarkable to need bolstering up with legends. He was a human mole, for ever burrowing underground. He began with a suite of three library rooms 78 yards long and originally lit by 1,100 gas jets. Then he started on a chapel, soon to be converted into a ballroom 55 yards by 22 yards. There were other rooms linked by long corridors along which ran a miniature railway designed to bring produce for underground banquets. He built above ground as well. There was a vast new riding house with cast iron columns, ranges of hot houses, an extension of the lake to three miles and more than 40 identical lodges.

Little of this is visible to the public, but there is one place where it is possible to have a glimpse of perhaps the most astounding of the Duke's subterranean works. At the extreme northern end of the estate, almost on the edge of Worksop, a long, unsignposted lane on the right of the main road turns back on itself and comes to an end by what looks like the mouth of a castellated railway tunnel, flanked by twin lodges. It is in fact the end of the Duke's 'escape' tunnel, brick-lined, a mile and a quarter long and wide enough for two carriages. The other end is in the coach house at Welbeck, where the Duke would begin his London journeys. When the coach passed through the tunnel mouth its green silk blinds were drawn and remained so even when Worksop station was reached. There the coach—with Duke— was lifted on to a flat railway truck and carried to London to be unloaded and driven, still with drawn blinds, through the streets of the capital.

It is perhaps odd that so shy a man should have wanted to visit London so often. Of various suggested explanations, none was so startling as that offered by Mrs Anna Maria Druce in 1897, 19 years after the Duke's death. In the press, and subsequently in various courts of law, she asserted that the Duke had lived a Jekyll-and-Hyde existence and that in his Hyde capacity he had been Thomas Charles Druce, a prosperous upholsterer in Baker Street, and, incidentally, her father-in-law, which made her eldest son the rightful Duke of Portland. Her case dragged on for several years until in 1907 the remains of T. C. Druce were exhumed, to the confusion of Mrs Druce who had believed his coffin to be empty.

The Duke may not have lived a double life, but his single one was peculiar enough. Living as a recluse in a suite of four or five rooms, he communicated with the outside world by means of two letter boxes, one for incoming messages and mail and the other for the outgoing. He rarely showed his face, even for his own shooting parties, and neighbours happening to meet him accepted that they should show no sign of recognition. Yet he is said to have conversed happily with any of the 15,000 workmen who for 18 years were employed in building his fantasy subterranean world at an annual cost of around £100,000, and whom he supplied with a donkey and umbrella each to ease their journey through the park. Indeed there is a theory that his building craze was prompted by a desire to keep down unemployment.

Much of our information about the fifth Duke comes to us from Lady Ottoline Morrell, the step-sister of the sixth Duke, and a remarkable character in her own right who seems to pop up in every literary biography of the early twentieth century. The sixth and seventh Dukes, and their Duchesses, have been—and still are—revered in Nottinghamshire, and beyond, for their philanthropy.

Worksop Manor, Welbeck's northern neighbour, has only history to offer the visitor, for it is not open to the public. The first house was built on the site in the late sixteenth century by Bess of Hardwick's fourth and last husband the Earl of Shrewsbury. One of its earliest visitors was Mary Queen of Scots, who was given there what Horace Walpole much later called a 'wretched little bed-chamber' by her gaoler-hosts. James I received far more sumptuous hospitality when he stayed there on his way south to assume the crown in 1603. In fact these nobles knew a thing or two about lavish hospitality, especially the Duke of Newcastle, who spent between £4,000 and £5,000 in entertaining Charles I to dinner at Welbeck in 1628 and nearly £15,000 on a longer later visit. They also knew several things about 'one-upmanship', and it was probably to keep ahead of the Newcastles that the Duke of Norfolk, after inheriting Worksop, planned to build there the largest mansion in Europe. His chance came after fire destroyed the earlier house in 1761. James Paine and an army of 500 workmen set to work two years later. But only one side of the proposed quadrangle had been completed when the Duke's nephew and heir died, and the work promptly stopped. The quarter of the house that was completed was 300 yards long, four storeys high and had 500 rooms. Ironically, this 'house that never was' passed by purchase in 1840 to the Clumber Duke of Newcastle who demolished it before reselling the estate. Worksop Manor today is mainly Victorian, with a few traces of the two earlier houses. Its history bears out Byng's comment of nearly two centuries ago that 'in these Duckeries (*sic*) there is an everlasting tide, one flows, another ebbs. . . .'

CHAPTER SIX

The Far North

Worksop bestrides the shallow valley of the River Ryton with one foot in the Dukeries and the other in the magnesian limestone country of north-west Nottinghamshire. On the strength of its Manor and nearly 4,000 acres of Clumber Park that lie within the borough, it should have been included in the previous chapter. The official guide places it 'in the heart of the Dukeries', but I would be inclined to agree with the pleasant wrought-iron sign that welcomes you to Worksop in describing it as the 'Gateway of the Dukeries', which is why I have rather brutally detached Manor from town and left the latter for this chapter.

Worksop, where it is tactful to remember that its Midland League football club once held mighty Tottenham Hotspur to a goalless draw in a Football Association Cup-tie but to forget that it lost the replay nine-nil, works and plays in two very different worlds. Having long since lost its traditional industry of liquorice making, it now finds work for half its adult male population in the local mines and the other half in a dozen or more varied industries, but it could evacuate them all with their families into the glades of the Forest within half an hour, if the need should ever arise. The borough arms recognizes this dichotomy by displaying, among other features, a miner's shovel and pick crossed and an uprooted oak tree. The crest, with two squirrels sitting back-to-back, and the supporters, a knight in armour and a forester holding a longbow, emphasizes the link with the Forest that is so obvious as you approach from the south.

If you come from the north, however, you get a rather different impression. You drive into a straggling, bustling town of 35,000 people that bears little resemblance to the 'pretty market town of two streets' that John Leland found in Henry VIII's reign, apart from the red sandstone mound called Castle Hill that may originally have been an ancient British earthwork. The castle itself was 'clene down' even in

Leland's day, but what is now the Old Ship Inn in the Market Place must have been built around the time of his visit. It has a jettied-out upper storey and a splendid array of sharply pointed gables. Bridge Street and Potter Street have some good Georgian buildings if you look above the modern shop fronts, as you have to do in most towns. Otherwise, apart from an impressive Jacobean-style railway station in the local Steetley stone, central Worksop is not architecturally memorable.

Yet just east of the centre—and linked to it by a modern Memorial Avenue that contains library, museum and hospital besides the war memorial—is the magnificent Priory Church of St Mary and St Cuthbert with its twin Norman towers and modern spire. This is almost all that remains of the Augustinian house originally known as Radford Priory. It was founded in 1103 by Henry de Lovetot, lord of the manor, just outside the old town of Worksop. Later in the same century the church was replaced by a larger building that must have resembled the present Southwell Minster, but of which only the nave (135-ft long) remains. The exquisite Lady Chapel was added about 1250, but after the dissolution this stood as an isolated, roofless shell until it was restored, and relinked to the nave by a new south transept in 1929. The bareness of the interior of the church probably reflects the vandalism that followed the suppression of the monastery, but there is a splendid late-twelfth century south door with elaborate iron scrollwork that must be among the earliest of its kind in England. A wall cabinet near the vestry door contains a grimmer relic: an arrow piercing a skull.

The only other surviving remnant of the Priory is its gatehouse, just south of the church. It is a delight. It has been called 'the most beautiful thing in Worksop', and there is no denying that. The lower portion, including the broad gateway, dates from the early-four-teenth century; the upper part, with its grand oriel window and the outside staircase, was added perhaps 50 years later. The interior was used as a school for many years, but after restoration it was reopened in 1973 to house a parish museum, the Citizen's Advice Bureau and the Council for Community Care, which seems an excellent way of using one of the county's smaller gems.

This part of Nottinghamshire has other treasures to offer the observant visitor. It is a stretch of rolling grassland, park-like in places, with patches of woodland on the Bunter outcrops, such as Treswell Wood, east of Retford, 118 acres of oak and ash woodland with an exceptional variety of scrub and herbaceous flora, that has survived intact from at least the reign of Edward the Confessor and has recently been bought by the Nottinghamshire Trust for Nature Conservation. Occasionally on the west, there are limestone walls to remind you that this is still magnesian limestone country with Yorkshire and the Derbyshire Peak not far away. In fact, the three counties meet within the borough of Worksop at Shireoaks, a colliery village that has now lost the oaks that once marked the boundary and can be avoided with no particular regret. It is more rewarding to drive north up the A60 and turn off left to visit the church of Carlton-in-Lindrick (the enclosure of the freedmen in the lime wood), the middle one of three adjacent Carlton villages.

This church is one of the oldest places of Christian worship in Nottinghamshire. In fact, in and around it, are three stones that suggest a pre-Christian origin. The 'Devil Stone', near the west front, was discovered in 1937. Legend has it that if you run round it seven times you either have good luck or see the devil, depending, apparently, on which way you run. Another stone above the fourteenth-century priest's door at the south end of the altar rail is a sun-stone, possibly used in pre-Christian worship. The grimacing demon over the gallery at the west end is the Green Man, that mysterious figure of English folk lore. Originally placed there to keep out other demons, he is now affectionately known locally as ''Orace'.

The church itself is basically early Norman, though the two lower stages of the tower, with a good deal of herring-bone work in the lower one, could be Saxon of two distinct periods. The tower was buttressed and topped with its battlements and eight pinnacles in the fifteenth century. The west doorway is late Norman and not in its original position, having been moved when the south aisle was added in 1831, but the tower arch again appears to be Saxon work with one side considerably earlier than the other, and there is a Saxon window high up in the chancel. There are many other features of note, such as the painted roof bosses over the plain Norman font; a twelfth-century stone altar that was found in 1939 buried under the high altar; and a lancet window in the Becket Chapel (restored 1967) containing what remains of the medieval stained glass from the east window after it had been deliberately smashed by the sacked coachman of a former rector. Altogether a church for the connoisseur, and not well known outside the area.

Just below the church, Carlton Mill stands on a small island, with the lake and dam behind and streams—one being the mill race—on either side. The attractive front was probably designed by the same Charles Battersby who built the nearby road bridge on which are inscribed his initials and the date, 1831, but parts of the mill are much older. It continued in use for grinding corn during the last war and has now been restored to working order. The mill and its small museum are open to the public on certain days in summer (two to five on Wednesday and Saturday afternoons at present, but it would be wise to check).

A short but pleasant walk from opposite the church leads to Wallingwells (formerly Walden-le-Wells in the park of Carlton-in-Lindrick), but nothing is left of the nunnery of St Mary, and only the coach house of the mansion where Lady Mary Wortley-Montagu stayed. To the east of Carlton, Hodsock is not so much a village as a very widely scattered series of farms and a priory that never was. The mansion called Hodsock Priory, once a home of the Clifton family and later of the Mellishes, is fairly modern, but it has a sixteenth-century brick gatehouse protected by a moat.

North Carlton and Langold are both planned colliery villages of interest mainly to students of industrial housing, and the same can be said of Harworth and Bircotes on the Yorkshire border to the north-east. As Styrrup has nothing much to offer besides a charming name and the sites of a Roman Villa and a medieval tilting ground, the sensible thing to do is probably to turn eastward onto the A634 at Oldcotes and head for Blyth. That way you cross Whitewater Common, which was a swamp until William Mellish drained it around 1770, and enter Blyth by an elegant balustraded bridge, another product of Mellish's enterprise.

Blyth is charming; quite the most beautiful village in north Nottinghamshire. Its centre round the triangular green has been declared a conservation area; at least two dozen of its buildings have been listed as being of architectural or historic interest, and it would be difficult to find an ugly one. Yet it may strike you as being rather a sad place. This is, in part, because it seems to have lost its *raison*

24. (opposite) *Southwell Minster, west front*

d'être. It is clearly an ancient market town and a route centre, indebted for the prosperity which it so manifestly enjoyed in Georgian times to its position within a horseshoe loop of the Ryton where the east-west road crossed the Great North Road. But within the last 20 years the whole road network in this district has changed its pattern, causing some confusion by a re-numbering of roads, and carrying what is now the A1(T)—which sounds much less romantic than the Great North Road—out of Blyth on a by-pass to the east. This change must have brought enormous benefits in terms of peace and quiet for the residents, and for visitors, the chance to stand and stare in some comfort at the warm red brick of the houses and their red pantiled roofs. But it has also brought that touch of melancholy that affects you when visiting a once-active friend in his retirement.

The other note of sadness will not be caught by those visiting Blyth for the first time. It is caused by the loss of the Hall, which after military occupation in the last war, simply degenerated into a hopeless ruin afterwards; now only its fine entrance gateway remains. Once the home of the Mellish family, local people who made money out of the Portuguese trade late in the seventeenth century and lost much of it gambling at Brooks' and Carlton House early in the nineteenth, it was when Celia Fiennes visited it in 1697, 'a very sweete House and Gardens and Grounds, it was of brick work coyn'd with stone and the Windows with stone all sashes . . . its in all parts a most compleate thing and its scituation most pleasant.' It had only just been rebuilt then and it was enlarged in the next century, a mere 50 years or so before the family had to sell it and move to Hodsock Priory.

The tomb and effigy of Edward Mellish, short, stout and bewigged, who built the 'fair and stately edifice . . .' are in the Priory Church that is Blyth's most dramatic and, in a way, saddest building. Sad because, as Pevsner says, 'the church is only a fragment of what it once was, and a sad, badly treated fragment at that', and because over the last 40 years or so its congregation and other friends have had to fight a long, hard and desperately expensive struggle to maintain what is left of this important building.

Its importance rests on its style and date. There has been a suggestion that it was built in the time of Edward the Confessor, but the fact is that it was started in 1088 when Roger de Busli founded the Benedictine Priory at Blyth. This would place it amongst the oldest

25. (opposite) *Southwell Minster. Late thirteenth-century carved foliage*

Norman work in England anyway, but the authorities seem to agree that its master mason followed a style that was already 30 or 40 years behind the times, based perhaps on the Abbey of Jumieges in Normandy. With its two aisles, transept, five apses and low central tower, the completed church rising out of a low landscape must have presented a majestic, if slightly chilling, sight, for enough remains to give you a sense of that majesty and, as Pevsner says, 'a feeling for early Norman grimness'.

Of the fabric, what remains is most of the nave, which now forms the north aisle. What happened was that about 1290 the Benedictines built a new south aisle as wide as the old nave and south transept put together, and this has become the nave and chancel of the present church. The west end of the old nave was replaced about 1400 by the splendid Perpendicular ashlar tower, its eight pinnacles jauntily joined by open-work cusped gables, that is such a prominent landmark for miles around. The eastern bays of the old nave were lost as the result of a dispute between monks and parishioners that resulted in a great wall being built across the church to divide nave from chancel. The cause of the quarrel has long been forgotten; the wall remains. After the dissolution everything east of it was demolished, except for the north aisle and eastern bays of the nave, the destruction of which would have jeopardized the rest of the structure. They became enclosed in the Hall gardens, and served for a time as an aviary, but in 1938 the eastern bay of the north aisle was reclaimed and became an additional vestry. The rest may be opened to the public eventually—when funds permit.

One other treasure in the church should be mentioned; the painting by Fra Bartolomeo (1490) of St Mary Magdalene that hangs on the north side of the high altar. And there are many more treasures in Blyth itself that compete for a word here; the former vicarage with its handsome cupola that William Mellish built close to the church in that productive year 1770; rows of cottages with Gothic windows; a dovecote; the old school, with its mullioned windows and old door; at least three coaching inns; the almshouses and the old hospital of St John, now Blyth's 'Spital Farm, to the south, near the junction of the old road and the new; these are just a few.

Two miles south-east of Blyth—but within the parish—Ye Olde Bell Hotel at Barnby Moor stands at the meeting point of the A634 and A638, which has shed most of its traffic load but is still marked on the map as the Great North Road. The Bell is not so much an hotel as a village in itself; one of those enormous coaching inns that warmed eighteenth-century travellers with huge log fires and steaming punch which were left to cool in the second half of the nineteenth century by travellers who went north by train, and revived in the twentieth century to serve modern comforts to a new generation of travellers who arrived in Bentleys and Jaguars.

That summarizes the history of the Bell. In 1792 a clergyman travelling for pleasure described it as 'the most comfortable and private public house, take it altogether, that I was ever at.' One of those who took it altogether was the sporting writer 'Nimrod' (Charles James Apperley) who travelled overnight from Huntingdon to reach the Bell for an eight o'clock breakfast. 'That was a still greater treat, for at no nobleman's house in the country could a better have been provided. When I was last there the celebrated Mr Clarke—celebrated for his breed of cattle and his horses, as well as for his larder and cellar—kept it, and I was glad to find that the reputation of the house was not about to suffer by the change of landlord, which is saying a good deal in this case.'

George Clarke, who kept the Bell from 1800 to 1842, left a large fortune, but his successor soon found himself with no post boys clamouring for their 60 beds and only an odd horse or two where there had been 120. The inn became a private house, which was later divided into two, and then another part became the village chapel. But early in the present century, when the roads again began to echo the rumble of wheels, the Bell re-opened and became in due course as well known as it was in 1805 when Pearce, the Game Chicken, made it his headquarters before and after his prize-fight at Blyth— sponsored by Colonel Henry Mellish—when he defeated the ageing Jem Belcher in the eighteenth round.

The road northward from Barnby Moor is quiet enough today to bring back some pleasure to main-road motoring. At commuter time on a summer evening, I met no more than a dozen cars before joining the trunk road south of Bawtry. Though a splendid road to drive on, it is not particularly attractive despite those magnificent Danish names: Barnby, Torworth, Ranskill and Scrooby, with Serlby and Scaftworth just off the road to west and east.

At Scrooby Top a lane runs off to the west to Serlby Hall, crossing on its way a mysterious earthwork that the Ordnance Survey calls Roman Bank but is more likely to be a Danish, or earlier, boundary. Serlby Hall is the northernmost of the Nottinghamshire houses that are shown to the public. The estate has been in the hands of the Monckton family since it was bought by John Monckton in 1722, five years before he was created Viscount Galway. He it was who called in James Paine to design the present red brick mansion in 1740. Paine tended to go for solidity, regularity and dignity rather than for show and this house follows his normal lines, though it pleasantly overlooks a spacious terrace and a lake and has a noble portico of Tuscan columns on the north front. The mansion was enlarged by the fourth Viscount in 1812, and by the seventh Viscount in this century.

It was the seventh Viscount who added the present entrance hall that contains the Galway State Coach, as well as a brass candlestick that belonged to General Wolfe, a reminder that Serlby was the home of General Robert Monckton who was Wolfe's second-in-command at the capture of Quebec. There are several letters to and from Wolfe in the house, and a fine portrait of General Monckton by Benjamin West hangs in the dining room under the beautiful relief plaster-work ceiling by Antonio Zucchi (1726–1795), the husband of Angelica Kauffmann. The diamond, enamel and ruby ring in the oak room was given to a pre-Serlby Monckton—Sir Philip—by Charles I on the battlefield of Marston Moor. A large Daniel Mytens portrait of that king and his queen, Henrietta Maria, is particularly interesting because it includes in a corner of the canvas the famous Court dwarf, Sir Geoffrey Hudson, himself an East Midlander, though from Rutland. That painting is in the drawing room, an elegant room with mainly French furnishings, and there and elsewhere in the house are other fine pictures, including portraits by that prolific pair Sir Geoffrey Kneller and Sir Peter Lely, who can seldom have had a moment to themselves.

The Great North Road avoids the centre of Scrooby by means of a bypass constructed with astonishing farsightedness about 150 years ago. It is a disappointingly unexciting village that looks as if it had seen better days, which indeed it did in the days when the Archbishops of York had a house there as a place of rest when travelling between York and London. Those days ended after Archbishop

Sandys, who died in 1588, devised a lease which somehow transferred the property into the hands of his family. Nothing now remains of this house in which Cardinal Wolsey stayed on his last northern journey, but close to its site is the manor farmhouse, which is one of several buildings in the village that have claims to having been the home of William Brewster, one of the leaders of the Pilgrim Fathers. There is no very clear evidence to support any of the claimants, any more than there is to say that he ever occupied Brewster's Pew in the church.

What is certain is that he held the office of 'Post' at Scrooby at a salary of 20d a day, later raised to two shillings—to which could be added such perquisites as letting out horses to private travellers—and that he entertained at his house from time to time some local followers of Robert Browne, who objected to certain principles of the Church of England, including episcopal ordination and the parochial system. Among these Brownists were the Rev Richard Clifton of Babworth, a few miles to the south, and William Bradford, from Austerfield, to the north. Brewster was thus well placed to act as host, and, wrote Bradford, 'with great love he entertained them when they came, making provision for them to his great charge'. The exact causes of their decision to seek refuge in the Low Countries are as obscure as much else in the Scrooby story. Brewster was certainly fined for recusancy, but whether that was the sole cause is uncertain. The rest of the tale of their attempted voyage from the Lincolnshire port of Boston; their eventual settlement first in Amsterdam and then Leyden, and finally their voyage in the *Mayflower* in 1620 is too well known to need recapitulation here.

One feature that must interest modern pilgrims to Scrooby, many of them American, is the unusual church tower that is square at the base and becomes octagonal below its battlements to match the fine spire.

Just north-west of the village is a rise still called Gibbet Hill, though the actual gibbet crumbled away in the 1830s. It was last used in 1779 to hang a local shepherd named John Spencer, who murdered the keeper of the turnpike gate nearby, and the gate-keeper's mother, with a hedge stake and took what money he could find. A little to the north-east the Ryton flows into the River Idle, which may live up to its unusual name today but was once extremely active. Until late in the eighteenth century it was the main trade highway for heavy goods such as lead from the Derbyshire mines and iron from the forges of Sheffield and Rotherham. They were carried, according to Defoe, in 'hoys, lighters, barges, or flat bottom'd vessels, out of its channel into the Trent. . . .'

The port of embarkation was Bawtry. It looks today an unlikely place to have been an inland port—though it has a Wharf Street and a modern-looking Ship Inn—with the Idle, sluggish and shallow, flowing through the meadows to the east. But it is still, as it was in 1724, 'a very well frequented place', and if it no longer 'stands upon the great post highway, or road from London to Scotland', it still appears to be full 'of very good inns and houses of entertainment'. It is a sort of transit camp, though a most elegant one, if you can imagine such a thing, with a fine Georgian posting inn and numerous other good buildings from that and earlier periods, in a splendidly wide main street that seems to be full of parked cars at all hours of day and night. Not all this traffic uses the A1, for Bawtry, conveniently sited between the Pennines to the west and the carrs, or fenland, to the east, is the meeting place of many roads and for many regular road-users. Long-distance lorry drivers and commercial travellers must be frequently meeting old friends there, in the same way that theatrical touring companies used to bump into other companies on the station platforms of York, Crewe or Bletchley.

But Bawtry, it must be admitted, is a few hundred yards outside Nottinghamshire in a narrow salient of the West Riding that extends to the Idle. Yet it is as difficult to omit from a book on Nottinghamshire as it is to miss it if you are motoring in these parts. In fact it is downright impossible to reach the extreme north-east of the county without driving through a portion of Yorkshire. Not that you may necessarily wish to do so, as neither of the two villages in this far-flung outpost of Nottinghamshire is particularly attractive. Finningley, the more northerly, looks like one of those large Fenland villages that string out along the road between Spalding and King's Lynn, and has been further disfigured by sand and gravel working. It has a large R.A.F. aerodrome, a level crossing that still opens for trains, and an interesting church with an oak pulpit of 1604 and a fine open-timbered roof. Sir Martin Frobisher, one of the greatest of the Elizabethan sailors, was once lord of the manor. A later landowner was Sir Cornelius Vermuyden, the Dutch drainage engineer, who worked on the draining of the carrs east of the village. Misson is a true fenland village, a bleak, isolated place, a mere 20 feet above sea level, on the north bank of the Idle and of interest only to anglers.

A much more attractive road out of Bawtry is the A631, once you are clear of the rather ugly railway viaduct just east of the town. Beyond the Idle, the site of a Roman fortlet to the north is more exciting on the map than on the ground. The first place of note is Everton, a biggish agricultural village with lots of those solid red brick farm buildings, so typical of north Nottinghamshire, strung out along the main road in the medieval style. There are others on the village street that runs north to the carrs, where more scattered farms stand on reclaimed land. The remains of a tower mill is another feature repeated in many a Nottinghamshire village, but the church is unusual in having a high, though short, nave and an early tympanum. 'Norman probably', says Pevsner, 'but of Viking descent; two horse-like dragons seemingly licking each other's muzzles in the friendliest spirit.'

At Drakeholes the road crosses the Chesterfield Canal and climb eastward on a stretch of road known locally and mysteriously as the 'Ramper' (Rampart perhaps?). The Chesterfield Canal was started by James Brindley and was completed after his death by his brother-in-law Hugh Henshall, in 1777. Following the valley of the Ryton through Worksop and then traversing the higher ground by means of four locks to the Idle valley at East Retford, it offered a more convenient and reliable outlet to the Trent for the lead, coal and iron of north Derbyshire and south Yorkshire than did the Idle, and so killed Bawtry as a river port. But its own active career was short-lived. In 1846, the canal company, having astutely translated the writing on the wall and formed their own railway company, joined forces with the Manchester, Sheffield and Lincolnshire Railway— an ancestor of the Great Central — and left the canal to look after itself. When I walked the canal bank from East Retford to Drakeholes Tunnel some 25 years ago I did not meet a soul on the towpath nor see a boat on the water. Today, more happily, the canal at Drakeholes is crowded with pleasure craft.

You catch a glimpse of some of these craft, and of the charming grounds of Wiseton Hall, as you climb up to Gringley-on-the-Hill on the A631. Gringley is a delightful surprise. Any hill in this part of Nottinghamshire is unexpected; Beacon Hill, at 255 ft is relatively a mountain at the end of a short, steep ridge on which Gringley perches, just off the main road. The village is attractive by any standards, with numerous fine houses and a good, mainly Perpendicular, church recently restored. Best of all about Gringley are its views, especially from Beacon Hill, a pre-historic hill fortress, where Prince Rupert later camped before relieving Newark. From there is the most astonishing view in the county. Eastward, on a clear day, you see Lincoln Cathedral, but the view north is what catches the imagination as you look out across mile after mile of the flattest, least occupied, least visited stretch of England; across the carrs, the Isle of Axeholme, Hatfield Moors, Hatfield Chase, and Thorne Waste to the distant Humber, with no land south of the Yorkshire Wolds higher than 30 feet.

You plunge down to the carrs (richly fertile except for the islands of peat) at Misterton, a bigger, older version of Misson, with nothing much for the visitor except that a church spire is rare in these parts. But West Stockwith is a must; a Trentside village that belongs to Holland rather than Nottinghamshire. When I saw it first, some 20 years ago, I had just returned from the Low Countries and I felt at once that I was still there. The winding, narrow streets, the brick tower mill converted into a private house with a projecting pitched roof, the deserted Chesterfield Canal basin with its wharfs and warehouses close to the mouth of the Idle, the quayside overlooking the tidal Trent, busy with commercial craft, all reminded me of those small ports on what was then the Zuider Zee. Best of all was the little red brick church of 1722, with its pretty bell-turret, built by the executors of William Huntingdon, 'a ship carpenter', whose life-size monument depicts him holding the drawing of a sailing ship, probably one of the many seagoing vessels that were built in the village in the eighteenth century. West Stockwith, which faces East Stockwith on the Lincolnshire bank of the Trent, has not changed much since my first visit, as it is mercifully outside commuterland, though it does become crowded with anglers at weekends.

Walkeringham and Beckingham are large villages standing back a mile or so from the Trent on the A161. Both have ancient Saxon names and good medieval churches containing interesting monuments. At Walkeringham Francis Williamson, who died in 1639, kneels to face his wife, also kneeling, as are their three children below. At Beckingham a brass plate engraved with a shipwreck scene is in memory of Marion Parkinson, one of only 190 survivors from the troopship *Birkenhead* that struck a rock off Cape Agulhas in 1852. She was the daughter of a drum major who was drowned. Her body lies in the cemetery near Beckingham church. This church also has a plain Norman tub font, but there are far more impressive Norman fonts in the neighbouring parishes of Saundby and Bole. The latter also has a good pulpit with four seventeenth-century Flemish panels, but tiny Saundby is the prettier village, with fine trees in and around the churchyard, including one splendid cedar with a trunk sixteen feet round. In an exclusively agricultural area the recently established cheese factory fits neatly into the environment in every sense.

When the road (now the A620) turns west on to higher ground away from the Trent Valley the scenery and the pattern of farming change. There are more trees, especially fruit trees, as you approach the Wheatleys. South Wheatley is so small that the wonder is not so much that its church is now a picturesque ruin as that it was ever built at all. North Wheatley is not particularly big either, but it is attractive and has in its Old Hall a wonderful example of decorative brickwork. Even the porch, with its Ionic pilasters, and the mullions and transoms in the windows are brick. The only stonework seems to be the date-stone of 1673 and the arms of the Cartwright family. The church is worth a visit too for its primitive oak staircase for the bellringers in the tower. It has 28 steps roughly trimmed from logs secured with wooden pegs to two beams, each over a yard wide near the top.

Anyone who is discouraged by Pevsner's dismissal of East Retford as 'a singularly unattractive town' can at least postpone a visit to this market centre by turning north on the edge of Clarborough and following a roughly pear-shaped detour along the rising ground on the flanks of the Idle valley. Clarborough and Clayworth are seen to best advantage from the Chesterfield Canal towpath. Both are straggling agricultural villages, but their sprawl is not unpleasant as it is at Hayton, between them, which is an absurd piece of subtopian ribbon building that should never have been allowed to happen.

Mattersey, on the other hand, is completely unsophisticated and rural, though it lost one of its chief attractions when its ancient three-arched bridge over the Idle collapsed in 1954. Fortunately, it still has the remains of its Priory, romantically sited on the west bank of the river a mile east of the village at the end of a rough track that is easier on the feet than on the springs of a car. The walk is pleasant, the site charming and the ruins evocative though sparse. Only the fragments of the church walls remain of the original buildings that were founded by Roger de Mattersey in 1185 for the Gilbertine canons, a small English Order that had no other house in the county. The monastery was destroyed by fire in 1279, and of its successor the best preserved parts are the two-aisled refectory, part of a cloister, and the south-east corner, though the ground plan has been exposed.

South of Mattersey the countryside has been marred by sand and gravel workings round Sutton and Lound, but Babworth is delight-fully wooded. Babworth is an odd place; a large parish in area con-taining church, Georgian Hall and beautiful cricket ground, all within the Hall grounds that Humphry Repton laid out; a toll-house serving as a post office on my last visit; but no village. This is now farther west in the former hamlet of Ranby that has grown alongside the new A1(T). The old Great North Road used to bisect the parish by Rushey Inn, now a row of cottages, where in 1503 Margaret Tudor, on her way north to marry James IV of Scotland, was enter-tained by the Aldermen of Retford, who paid 12s. 11d. for wine, ale and two minstrels. If these dignitaries of Retford felt that the money might have been more sensibly spent in their own town they left it to a later generation to have the road diverted to their advantage. This was done by Act of Parliament in 1766, to the great delight of the townsfolk, whose descendants were still more delighted to lose the road again just over two centuries later.

East Retford, which swallowed West Retford, on the other side of the Idle, in 1878, is not quite as black as Pevsner paints it. There are a few Georgian buildings to see above modern shop fronts and the over-restored parish church looks impressive at a distance. Historically the town has two claims to distinction of a sort. It still has a Lord High Steward, though now without the responsibilities vested on him in the Middle Ages, and it retains a certain wry pride in remembering its numerous dishonourable mentions in the 1832 Reform Bill debates. After the election of 1826 brought notoriety to this 'ancient and corrupt borough' it lost its right to return two Members to Parliament and those of its electors who had voted for the winning candidates lost the right to collect the customary 40 guineas each.

A more violent political battle is recalled by the inscription on a gravestone in Elkesley churchyard, south of Retford, which records that 'John Baragh, gentleman, was murdered by Midford Hendry, officer of the Guards.' The incident took place in 1721 in the Jockey House Inn (now a farmhouse) on the old Great North Road as the result of an over-heated political argument. A more interesting spectacle at Elkesley might be the meeting of the Maun, Meden and Poulter to form the Idle, but as this takes place at a busy road junction it is hardly a sight to savour. The next parish, Gamston, has a pleasing looking church with a splendid tower and rood turret but a dull interior restored by Sir George Gilbert Scott in 1855. The rectory was the birthplace in 1781 of Henry Fynes Clinton, a noted classical scholar with a taste for statistics. In his daily journal, religiously kept in Latin or Greek, he recorded that he read 5,223 pages of Greek literature in his seven years and eight months at Oxford.

The most interesting churches hereabouts are in the Markhams, East and West, which have three between them of vastly different types. East Markham is almost pure fifteenth-century Perpendicular, light and roomy, with large nave, almost equally large chancel and an imposingly tall tower arch. An alabaster tomb-chest to Sir John Markham, who died in 1409, has historic as well as visual interest as he was the Judge Markham who drew up the document for deposing Richard II. His son John became Lord Chief Justice in Edward IV's reign. An outstandingly good and large brass in the floor of the south aisle is of the first Sir John's widow who later married William Mering. This church is a must, full of good things. All Saints, West Markham (sometimes called Markham Clinton) is almost equally appealing in a totally different way. Lying in a slight hollow among the orchards, it is a truly rural, somewhat primitive, church. Its weatherboarded west turret and half-timbered gable above a stone porch suggest an Essex rather than a Nottinghamshire setting. The porch shields a Norman doorway on which an old oak door is said to hang on its original hinges. Inside is an unusually interesting Norman font, three old carved roof bosses, and some oak benches of similar antiquity. Naturally there is less to see than in its larger neighbour, but it is remarkable that there is anything at all, since it was compulsorily closed and left to rot for over a century, from 1831.

The reason for this emerges if you drive half a mile up the quiet road to the hamlet of Morton. After a short distance the road changes character to become a dignified avenue that seems to have strayed from the Dukeries, leading very soon to a classical Grecian temple that might sit comfortably in the borough of St Marylebone but looks incongruous in rural north Nottinghamshire. This combined church and mausoleum was designed by Sir Robert Smirke, architect of the British Museum, to house the tomb of Georgiana Elizabeth, Duchess of Newcastle, who died in 1822 at the age of 33 in giving birth to twins, her thirteenth confinement. Her husband, the fourth Duke, possibly using the money received in compensation for the burning of Nottingham Castle, spared no expense on his church and when it was completed in 1831 he ensured that it should be fully used by closing All Saints and transferring its congregation there. Any protest at such arrogance would no doubt have been met with the same indignant, 'Can't I do what I like with my own?' that he uttered after evicting 40 of his Newark tenants for voting against his candidate in the 1831 election.

The social revolution that has taken place since the days of this impossible Duke are epitomized at West Markham, where it is the less pretentious church that has been restored to life and the Duke's left to crumble away into disuse. To be fair, though, it would have been a pity if disintegration had been complete. In its own urban style it is an interesting church (despite a rather depressing interior) with a pompous Doric portico and rotunda, and worth preserving for its curiosity value anyway. So it is pleasing to be able to record that a rescue operation has begun. But one wonders what the Duke would have thought of the kennels and cattery next door to his mausoleum.

Tuxford, two miles to the south, is a large, pleasant village that seems to have cheerfully survived a disastrous fire in 1702, the loss of its market, and the fact that it is now literally overlooked by the Great North Road, built on an embankment, where traffic roars above the village. There are reminders of its lost status in the handsome Newcastle Arms, built just after the fire, in what is still called the Market Place, and in the old grammar school, founded in 1669, now a branch library and looking virtually unchanged as though heeding the stone inscription above the main entrance; 'What God hath built let no man destroy.' With its hipped roof and dormer windows, this is one of the most attractive small buildings in the area.

West of Tuxford a short run brings you back to the Dukeries, but a slight detour through the lanes to the north avoids the grim eastern approach to Ollerton and enables you to see Haughton and Botham-sall. Not that there is much of Haughton to see; just a few scattered farms. One of them, Haughton Hall Farm, stands on the site of one of Smythson's Elizabethan mansions, abandoned by the Hollies family when they moved to Welbeck. It was the birthplace in 1599 of Denzil Hollies, one of the five Members whom Charles I tried to arrest. Close to, by the Maun, are the roofless remains of the Norman church that became the domestic chapel of the family.

Most of the evidence would suggest that Bothamsall could be eminently avoidable. Its name sounds like the invention of a Lanca-shire comedian, its church of 1845 is dismissed by Pevsner as 'just a piece of imitation Notts Perp', it has within the parish a Coal Board training centre, one of Britain's latest and largest collieries and at least two oil wells. But the reality is quite different. True, the church has a curiously pinched tower, but the village is compact and attrac-tive in a delightful setting on a shelf above the meadows, through which the Meden and Maun flow on almost parallel courses a few hundred yards apart, actually meeting briefly under a screen of ash and alder at a spot west of the village called Conjure Alders. Where they separate again, a splendid tree-dotted, dry-moated mound of a Norman castle commands the Meden valley at the approach to the village. The colliery, not unhandsome anyway, is nearer to the hamlet of Bevercotes whose name it takes. The training centre at Lound Hall contains a mining museum which was officially opened to the public in September 1972 and has some interesting exhibits, of which the largest is the pitch pine tandem headgear from Brinsley that featured in the film version of *Sons and Lovers*. At present the museum is open on the first Sunday afternoon in each month from 2 to 5.30 (or dusk in winter), and on certain Bank Holidays, but these hours will be extended as the museum become more established.

And the oil wells? They are not what you expect, even if you do expect oil wells in Britain at all. In fact Britain (excluding the North Sea) produced over 82,000 tons of oil in 1970, of which nearly half came from Nottinghamshire. But that was less than one tenth of the 1943 production when the need to exploit our own oil was vital. The greater part of that came from Nottinghamshire, chiefly from

Eakring, south of Ollerton in the Keuper country, where oil was struck in the county for the first time in 1939, just at the right time. The Bothamsall finds came as late as 1958. The wells are quite unobtrusive, with none of the traditional derricks, nor the hustle and bustle that you might expect; just a small horizontal black pump nodding its head up and down like some particularly absurd donkey; no untidy buildings; no men working. Some of these wells are in corn fields. In one just west of Bothamsall the corn was being cut round the well as I passed, the combine harvester looking far larger and more menacing than the pump. It was one of those rather bizarre sights that you somehow come to accept as normal in Nottinghamshire.

CHAPTER SEVEN

North and West of Trent

Between the Dukeries and the Trent valley the Keuper sandstone and marl country stretches down to the northern outskirts of Nottingham. It is the type of country that the geographers usually describe as 'gently undulating', tilting gradually from about 350 ft in the west to around 150 ft in the east, but the tilt is not really obvious on the ground any more than the undulations are always gentle, as a retired carter made clear to me in describing a terrifying winter journey up Oxton Hill. That, of course was with horses and cart, and the motorist is unlikely to find the occasional 'steep hill' sign any more than a refreshing change after the gentle gradients of the Dukeries and the north. Equally refreshing is the scarcity of major roads. South of the Ollerton-Tuxford road, only two A roads cross from west to east until one is almost in Nottingham, and only a single one runs north and south; even that goes no farther north than Southwell and marks the extreme eastern limit of the area.

All this must be frustrating for the thrusting motorist, but he is, happily, a rare visitor to this area. There is little to attract him. The only town is Southwell, with a population of under 5,000, which is a good deal less than that of many overgrown villages to the west. There are only two recognized 'places of interest' and one of those is rather too specialized—and too remote—to lure the average sight-seer. The villages are small, widely separated and just too far out of Nottingham to entice the commuters. So a pattern of minor roads that evolved in the horse and cart era is perfectly adequate for the motorist in no particular hurry and for the tractor driver whose pace is necessarily restricted.

This is one of the great charms of the Keuper country. It is one of those rare regions which has not yet sacrificed its all to the great god car; where the lanes twist and turn with apparent inconsequence but in fact to conform with a medieval field-pattern; the occasional straight stretch with a wide grass verge owes its directness to the enclosure commissioners of the eighteenth century rather than to the Transport Ministers of the twentieth. For this is a working countryside. Nottinghamshire has nearly 400,000 acres under crops and grass and some of the best corn and sugar beet grows on the red, marly soil hereabouts.

It is also, in its own unpretentious way, a beautiful countryside. Not everybody may agree. Beauty lies in the eyes of the beholder, and to this beholder it has a fresh, unspoilt charm that is sometimes lacking in more widely publicized beauty spots. Like some pictures; some girls for that matter; you have to look several times before you begin to appreciate the subtleties of colour and configuration that give character and charm. Some people may think it tame because—like most of our English country—it has been tamed by man and farmed by him for perhaps a thousand years. But though man is capable of committing atrocities on the landscape he is also capable, with equal absence of intent, of laying down patterns of fields, woods and occasional buildings that fit perfectly into the natural framework. It sounds horribly banal to call it typically English countryside, but the exile will understand what I mean; it is the sort of landscape for which I used to yearn during wild middle watches in mid-Atlantic in the winter of 1940; the sort of landscape that Constable painted.

In recent years the face of this stretch of country has changed slightly because, as elsewhere, some of the hedges have been grubbed up, giving it in places a medieval rather than an eighteenth-century pattern. And there is one place, Laxton, which has retained its medieval character without major interference from eighteenth-century enclosure commissioners.

Laxton is not particularly easy to find. The best approach is southward from Tuxford. This way is direct and has the additional merit of passing through Egmanton, which is worth a short stop. A stream runs through the village, as at Linby, and there are chestnuts and yews round a church that should delight disciples of Sir John Betjeman because of its colourful screen, pulpit, organ case and east window by Sir Ninian Comper, dating from a restoration of 1897–8 that enhanced the beauty of this ancient church rather than

26. (opposite, above) *Newark Castle*

27. (below) *Trent Bridge, Newark, with the chimneys and gables of Ossington Coffee Palace beyond*

disfiguring it, as happened too often elsewhere. This is a church that really should be seen, but the motte-and-bailey castle is as disappointing as most Nottinghamshire castles, being no more now than the inevitable green mound.

As it happens, Laxton has perhaps the best surviving example in the county of this type of Norman castle, for it is possible to see the remains of a dry moat and a little of the ground-plan. But even that is precious little, though the short grassy walk from opposite the church is worth taking for its own sake and also because of the pleasant view of the village from the castle mound. However, Laxton's castle is just a slight bonus. Its main attraction—especially for the economic historian—lies in the survival of its open field system of agriculture. 'There have been inclosures of fields in the remoter parts of the parish, to make compact farms', says C. S. and C. S. Orwin, in *The History of Laxton*, 'but the three open fields remain, unique in England, with their scattered holdings, their common grazing, and their manorial court, a living example of the social and economic life which prevailed, in the greater part of the country, back through the centuries to days so remote that its origin is lost in antiquity.'

Just why this system should have survived uniquely at Laxton is uncertain, but what is certain is that the system will endure under the Minister of Agriculture, who is now lord of the manor. And there are the three great fields, clearly marked on the one-inch map: West Field, Mill Field and South Field, each of about 300 acres. On the ground, admittedly, they are not quite so easy to comprehend. The unobservant traveller might pass through Laxton without really grasping the significance of what he was seeing. Only from the air does it become quite clear.

The fields are divided into strips of various sizes, averaging about three and a quarter acres, distributed among the various tenants, though recent consolidation has formed some larger individual holdings. Yearly, in rotation, one field is sown to wheat, one to other crops and the other left fallow. After the crop has been gathered the field is thrown open for common grazing. The stretches of meadow called sikes (pronounced 'six') at the ends of the furrows are let by auction each midsummer, the successful bidder having the right to cut the grass for hay.

The system is administered by the manorial court, the Court Leet,

28. (opposite) *St Mary Magdalen, Newark, showing high altar, reredos and east window*

which meets annually at the summons of the Bailiff and is presided over by the Steward. It appoints a jury drawn from the tenants and freeholders whose duty is to inspect the fields to see that boundaries are being observed, ditches cleared and the customs of the manor generally observed, defaulters being duly fined. After the perambulation the juries have lunch, the newest member paying for the beer. The records of the Court go back to 1651, but the Court itself was meeting for centuries before then.

The layout of the village, as might be expected, also follows the medieval pattern. There are few outlying farms, as these were a development that followed enclosures. Most of the inhabitants live in the two compact village streets. The farm houses are on narrow strips of land and often present a gable end to the street to save space. The farm buildings are adjacent, the kitchen garden and orchard behind, with a croft farther back. It is a layout still fairly common in rural Nottinghamshire, even in villages ringed around with post-enclosure farms.

The church of St Michael the Archangel stands proudly on a rise at the junction of the two streets, its magnificent nave clerestory of about 1490 making it externally one of the most pleasing churches in Nottinghamshire. That it is internally less satisfying is the result of the usual eighteenth-century neglect—when the interior was littered with rubbish—followed by an insensitive restoration which shortened the nave to rebuild the tower and thus destroyed the proportions of nave and chancel. But it is still an interesting interior, with a portion of a beautiful screen in the north aisle given by Robert de Trafford, Vicar of Laxton, in 1532. The monuments of the de Everingham family, lords of Laxton from the thirteenth to the fifteenth century are poorly preserved, but the oak effigy of Adam de Everingham's second wife is noteworthy in being the only surviving wooden medieval effigy in the county. Two other features of the church that appealed to me were the old plough in the churchyard and the most interesting exhibition of village history, the work of the local school children, in the south aisle. It might be a good idea if every church contained a permanent exhibition like this.

From Laxton an inconsequential lane wanders westward to the hamlet of Moorhouse and then turns sharply southward to Ossington, still the home of the talented Denison family, though the Georgian

Hall that they occupied for almost two centuries was demolished in 1963. The most famous Denison was John Evelyn (1800–73), Speaker of the House of Commons 1857–72 and subsequently Viscount Ossington. He was one of a remarkable band of brothers, nine in all, from their father's second marriage. Five obtained Firsts at Oxford and all had distinguished careers, one becoming Bishop of Salisbury and another Governor-General of Australia. (It is worth recording that of the 15 children of the father's two marriages, all but two survived infancy, a high proportion for that era.) But probably none of these worthy Denisons can have been as colourful as their forebear, William, who bought the Ossington estate in 1768. Descendant of a long line of Leeds clothiers, he followed his father in developing an export trade to Portugal, Italy and the Netherlands, an occupation so time-consuming that he was never able to discharge the duties of Mayor of Leeds to which he was four times elected, and so profitable that he was able to buy ten large but rundown estates in four counties. These he improved by remote control, relying at Ossington mainly on frequent letters of instruction to his head woodman and, rather surprisingly, the curate. It is a tribute to their diligence and his force of personality that the estate that he bought for £34,000 was estimated to be worth £60,000 ten years later; at a period of only mild inflation.

William Denison died in 1782, leaving half a million pounds at a conservative estimate, and his brother and heir, Robert, immediately commissioned John Carr of York to build a church in his memory. It is worth visiting for the life-size statues of the brothers by Nollekens. The ship that is carved in relief—along with wool bales and sheep— on the base of William's statue, does not necessarily confirm the local tradition that much of his fortune came from the sale of the cargo in a ship of his that happened to be the first to reach Lisbon after the earthquake of 1755.

Norwell (originally Northwell, as distinct from Southwell) has lost, in addition to part of its name, its market and fair, its three prebends of Southwell and its six moated houses, though several of the moats are visible. The church is worth visiting, as is the one at Caunton, which lies attractively on a little stream simply called the Beck. Hugh Hole was vicar in 1567 and his descendants still live at Caunton Grange. In the churchyard is the grave of Samuel Reynolds Hole, better known as Dean Hole. Squarson of Caunton before becoming

Dean of Rochester, he is remembered as one of the most prolific, skilful and literate amateur rose growers of all time. In 1851, he recorded, he had over 1,000 trees and more than 400 varieties of roses, and he wrote most charmingly about them.

Caunton lies just off the Newark-Ollerton road that runs along a narrow ridge and is worth following at least as far as Kneesall, whose splendid fifteenth-century church tower is an outstanding landmark. The tower has angels instead of gargoyles. A fragment of an Anglo-Saxon shaft is dismissed by Pevsner as 'nothing special', but Hall Farm nearby is said by M. W. Barley to be one of the earliest brick houses in Nottinghamshire. Though much altered, it still bears traces of its origin, probably in the sixteenth century when it is likely that bricks from the Low Countries were being imported to East Coast ports.

A quieter road from Caunton follows the Beck valley, passing the park of Beesthorpe Hall that Capability Brown laid out, to Maplebeck, as pretty as its name. The quaint village pub—called The Beehive and not much bigger than one—is probably sufficiently remote to escape 'development' from ham-fisted brewing moguls.

West of Maplebeck is Eakring, which despite being the centre of the Nottinghamshire oil field and an outpost of a Nottinghamshire-based battery-egg empire, has retained its rural atmosphere almost intact. It is sad that this village is chiefly known for its disgraceful treatment of a former rector, the Rev William Mompesson. He went to Eakring in 1670 from Eyam, the Derbyshire village which lost 267 of its 350 inhabitants in the Great Plague of 1665–66. The disease had been carried from London in a parcel of clothing, but Mompesson prevented it from spreading farther by persuading his parishioners to stay within the parish boundaries. When he moved to Eakring he was entitled to expect a hero's welcome, but ironically, his new flock refused to allow him to stay in the village for fear of infection. He was obliged to live in a hut in Rufford Park and to hold services under an ash tree just outside the village. The tree was destroyed by lightning years ago, but a stone cross marks the site of what was later called Pulpit Ash and a young ash has been planted nearby. Mompesson seems to have lived down the early prejudice, for he remained at Eakring—and became a Prebendary of Southwell—until his death in 1708. He is commemorated in Eakring church, rather inadequately.

Southward is Kirklington, which has a water-mill, a Georgian Hall with nineteenth-century trimmings (now a school) in a sizeable park, and a church with a seventeenth-century brick tower. Otherwise the most interesting thing about the church, dedicated to St Swithin, is the story of a sporting vicar in the last century, who used the wooden pulpit as a portable screen for duck shooting. The modern stone pulpit offers far less scope.

The obvious thing now is to make for Southwell by any one of several pleasant routes. As good a way as any is to walk along the disused railway track from Farnsfield which the Nottinghamshire County Council has sensibly converted into a footpath. It is no ruck-sack-and-heavy-boots walk, but an easy stroll of five miles (half that if you join the track south of Kirklington) that enables you to get the feel of a gentle stretch of country and puts you in the right mood for exploring Southwell. But the motorist can acquire the same sort of relaxed atmosphere by a leisurely drive through the orchard country round Edingley and Halam, with a short stop in the latter village. Not that Halam has many obvious tourist attractions; a small church with a squat, sturdy tower that looks like one of those defence-obsessed church towers of the Welsh border; splendid Norman chancel arch; a church bell that has rung each Sunday since Plantagenet times; a dovecote of Tudor bricks with a pyramidial roof in the grounds of Halam House; that is about all. Yet Halam grows on you somehow, probably because of its extraordinary dreamlike peace-fulness.

You get this same feeling even more strongly in Southwell, a place straight out of Trollope. I say 'place' because nobody seems quite sure if it is a city, town or village. Technically it is a village, though it offers all the services to be expected of a town, including good car parking and hotel accommodation—to place them in what now seems to be the correct order. And, of course, its Minster would grace any city and has been a cathedral since the Southwell Diocese was formed in 1884. As James I is said to have exclaimed, on passing through the town on his way south to the throne in 1603, 'By my blude this kirk shall justle with York or Durham or any other kirk in Christendom', which the *New Yorker* might dismiss as one of those exclamations that probably never got exclaimed, but would certainly have been justified. An early twentieth-century writer made the same point more neatly in saying, 'Other churches may be older, a few may be larger, but none are more beautiful.'

We had better take the question of age first. Nobody knows the date of the first church at Southwell. What is reasonably sure is that Oskytel, Archbishop of York, established—or re-established—a church in 956. By the time of the Norman Conquest this was a Collegiate Church or Minster served by a body of priests called a College—supported by prebendal endowments of land or tithes. These prebendaries were secular canons, free to work in their own parishes. Thus Southwell was never a monastic establishment. In a sense it was a kind of sub-cathedral, looking after the needs of the southern areas of the large see of York as the similar collegiate foundations of Ripon and Beverly did for the west and east, and this function did not cease until the College was dissolved in 1840.

Nothing of the early church stands today, but there is a fragment of tessellated paving below the pews in the south transept and a Saxon tympanum now used as a lintel over a doorway of the west wall of the north transept. In addition, some pre-Conquest carved and mouldered stones were discovered and re-used during the nineteenth-century repair operation.

The church you see today belongs mainly to three building periods. First there is the nave, crossing, transepts and western towers, started under Archbishop Thomas II of York (1108–14) and completed within about 50 years. Then came the east end from about 1234–48, and finally the chapter house of 1290 or thereabouts. Since then there has been no major building work, though there have been minor repairs and restorations in every century. These were particularly necessary after Parliamentary soldiers had stabled their horses in the Minster and committed other acts of vandalism. The west spires were removed in 1801 because the towers were considered unsafe, but Ewan Christian put back new spires of similar design in 1880 and also designed the waggon roof in timber for the nave, the original one having been destroyed by fire in 1711.

There is not the space here to attempt a description of the Minster. Anyway, you must see it for yourself. I can only pick out a few points that seem to me outstanding. First the Norman nave, crossing and transept, which have been called 'one of the most perfect examples of Romanesque building in England'. One cannot say more. If you go there from Blyth you cannot help noting what a difference a few years made in the refinement of Norman architecture. The pillars are no less massive, but serenity has replaced grimness. There is serenity too in the chancel, but the difference in style is astonishing. This is Early English architecture at its most English. But perhaps the most captivating bit of the Minster is the chapter house, small, octagonal, light, and unique in England in being stone-vaulted in one span without a central pier. Every boss on its arched ribs is carved in a variety of natural foliage. It is the naturalness of the carvings that catch the eye. These were surely the work of men who, like Thomas Hardy, 'noticed things', the work perhaps of local men from Sherwood Forest who knew about nature. And they knew, too, about people. The heads round the chapter are surely real people, probably the workmen themselves. There is the master mason, and a man with toothache. There are similar heads on the slightly later choir screen: a man pulling at his beard; another scratching his leg. You get the feeling that the men who did these carvings at Southwell were happy in their work, and some of that happiness must surely have been transmitted to generations of later visitors.

The Minster stands in a charming churchyard flanked at a respectful distance by agreeable buildings, with two groups within the precincts that command attention. On the south side are the ruins of the old palace of the Archbishops of York, parts of which are incorporated in the residence of the Bishop of Southwell, called the Bishop's Manor and built in 1907. The old palace—some pedants argue that it was a country retreat rather than an official palace—dates mainly from the fifteenth century. Wolsey, when out of favour, spent some months there and complained bitterly of the expense of its upkeep. Cromwell's troops knocked it about pretty savagely and when they had left the local inhabitants indulged in further vandalism. It has been a ruin ever since. The Vicars' Court, at the east end of the churchyard, is a delightful group of five beautifully proportioned Queen Anne brick houses with hipped roofs. There are two on each side of a lawn divided by a paved path. They were built for the Vicars Choral by the College of prebendaries around 1702. The third side of the courtyard at the end of the path is occupied by the Provost's official residence. The whole group, though smaller and less ancient than the Vicars' Close at Wells is nearly as satisfying.

Though the town is dominated by its great church as totally as say, Sherborne and Wimborne are by theirs, it still has other good things to offer. There is the Saracen's Head, for instance, 'a coaching inn, with an unpretentious long, cottagey seventeenth century front' as Pevsner so aptly describes it, which has absorbed the Assembly Rooms, built by a prolific local architect, Francis Ingleman, in 1807. A peep through the archway leading to the courtyard reveals a scene that can hardly have changed since that May morning in 1647 when King Charles 1 and his 'plain-dealing chaplain', Dr Hudson, rode in and dismounted after what was to be the King's last ride as a free man. There, tired after riding hard through the night from Stamford, they found waiting for them, Montreuil, the French envoy, who had been acting as intermediary between Charles and the Scottish Commissioners. In the inn, after the King had rested, there were more talks; the Commissioners were summoned from their lodgings in the Archbishop's Palace to dine with him. They, according to Hudson, 'desired him to march to Kellum for security. Wither we went after dinner'. From Kelham Hall, between Southwell and Newark where the Scottish army had its temporary headquarters, the King was taken north and later sold to Parliament for £400,000.

Ironically, The Saracen's Head was then called by its old name, the King's Head, as it still was when Oliver Cromwell spent a night or two there not long afterwards. The irony of it may have occurred to somebody early in the next century when the present name was adopted.

A little way north of the Saracen's Head, overlooking the pleasant Burgage Green, is a Georgian house with a four-pillared porch. This is Burgage Manor, where Byron stayed with his mother in vacations from Harrow and Cambridge between 1804 and 1807. Boredom comes easily to an adolescent, so it is not surprising that to Byron, Southwell was 'the region of dulness itself', except, apparently, when he was playing the lead in amateur dramatics and flirting, according to the local gossips, with a Miss Julia Leacroft. Four years later he was recommending the place in words not unlike those used by John Byng in 1789 when he had called it 'a well-built clean town such a one as a quiet distressed family ought to retire to'. That is still true.

The Nottingham road rises gently out of Southwell past the Nottinghamshire Farm Institute at Brackenhurst Hall, where farming techniques are taught. From this road you get fine views back over grassland and orchards to where the graceful cruciform Minster, with its tower and twin spires, dwarfs the little town and its attractive ancient satellites of Westhorpe and Easthorpe. It was at Easthorpe, in the garden of a Mr Bramley, that a young apple tree produced, around 1800, the first crop of that now famous Bramley Seedling. The original tree, now recumbent, can still be seen in the garden.

Just beyond Brackenhurst a narrow lane on the right leads to Halloughton, which is much more exciting than one would expect of a tiny scatter of houses with no village centre. The excitement chiefly hinges on the white-fronted Manor House opposite the church. It is a medieval house with a built-in tower, presumably for defence, something rare in the East Midlands, and was built for a prebendary of Southwell. Farther on, just before the lane peters out beyond a stream, Manor Farm has been attractively modernized and has handsome, cheerfully colourful outbuildings. Beyond them a footpath leads to Halloughton Dumble. Dumbles are simply dingles, steep-sided valleys usually overgrown with gorse and brambles. They are numerous in the area, and popular with picnickers who are prepared to stretch their legs to find them.

At Thurgarton the road drops down to the foot of the Keuper ridge and continues along the edge of the Trent Valley. But the position of the churches at Thurgarton and Lowdham indicate that these were villages of the Keuper whose lands stretched down into the valley, where the houses are almost exclusively modern. Thurgarton Church stands on rising ground and looks like an uncompleted reproduction of Southwell Minster. It is in fact all that is left—'a terribly mangled fragment', as Pevsner puts it—of the Augustinian priory that Ralph D'Aincourt set up in the twelfth century. The church was built about 1230 and may have rivalled Southwell in size and magnificence, as the surviving west tower and doorway suggest. But the other tower has gone, the chancel is Victorian and the interior of the church is both dark and out of proportion. Not all the trouble resulted directly from the Dissolution. The Coopers, who acquired the site, apparently did little harm for more than two centuries, and then in 1777 John Gilbert Cooper made up for it by demolishing the south-west tower of the church and what was left of the other priory buildings. On the site he erected a red brick house. It is quite a good house—the Georgians hardly ever put a brick wrong—and it became from 1884 to 1909 the residence of the Bishops of Southwell. But it is in the wrong place. Crouched up against the stone walls of the church it is ludicrous. John Gilbert Cooper was something of a literary man; Johnson called him, with some justification, 'The Punchinello of Literature'. He wrote a book called *Letters on Taste*; but he evidently never read it.

Just off the main road beyond Thurgarton is Gonalston, a pretty, leafy, cottagey village, somewhat marred by too many aggressive notices on red boards intended to deter trespassers but much more likely to incite reprisals. A smithy of 1845 has this verse on horseshoe-shaped brickwork:

> *Gentlemen as you pass by*
> *Pray on this shoe cast your eye*
> *If it is too tight We'll make it wider*
> *T'will ease the horse and Please the Rider*
> *If lame by Shoeing (as they sometimes are)*
> *You can have them eased with the greatest care.*

Close to the main road, at the side of the lane leading southward from the village, the ruins of a red brick three-storey mill straddles the narrow, shallow stream called the Dover Beck. Visitors are clearly unwelcome, but the mill can be viewed satisfactorily from the lane. The iron water-wheel is still in position, but a chimney suggests that there was not always enough water to work the wheel. The mill is almost certainly Lambert's cotton mill to which an orphan named Robert Blincoe was sent at the age of seven in 1822, along with other apprentices from St Pancras poor house in London. Blincoe wrote an account of the four years he spent there, working an average of 14 hours a day, six days a week, 'continually being beaten, pulled by the hair of his head, kicked or cursed'. He made one attempt to escape, but was caught at Burton Joyce and punished severely on his return to the mill. But when the mill closed and he was transferred to another in Derbyshire he found conditions there even worse.

A quiet road flanked by wide grass verges and horse chestnut trees leads north from Gonalston to Epperstone, which Firth aptly described as 'one of the daintiest little villages in the county.' Thirty years later, Pevsner found it 'uncommonly pleasing', and so it is today. Its tree-lined village street slopes gently up from a tributary of the Dover Beck, with a square red brick dovecote on the left just below the

Manor House, which has a crumbling Tudor doorway set in the wall close to its main gates. Opposite, the church stands high above the road, with the unspoilt Cross Keys inn just below. From the car park behind the inn there is a pleasing view of red-soiled fields sloping down from a ridge crowned by elms, a lofty poplar and two fine copper beeches. The parish footpaths are still perambulated each Rogation Sunday, the walkers being rewarded with tea in the village hall. Epperstone won a 'best-kept village' award in 1971, without apparently stooping to that over-zealous housewifely pernicketiness that sometimes mars these otherwise admirable competitions.

Farther north still, on the eastern edge of Sherwood Forest, Oxton is possibly even more beautiful because of the parkland in which it lies, the wealth of handsome, dignified red brick houses of the seventeenth and eighteenth centuries and its curious air of timelessness. Like many other rural Nottinghamshire villages, its population declined between 1850 and 1950, so that the signs of new development at one end of the village are not unwelcome, so long as they are not allowed to spread too far. In the attractive church that has something from each century from the twelfth to the twentieth—and a yew tree in the churchyard 600 years old—are hatchments of the Sherbrookes, lords of the manor since Elizabethan times. Two White Ensigns at the west end were flown in ships commanded by Sherbrookes of Oxton; one in the First World War by Captain Henry Sherbrooke, D.S.O., R.N., and the other in the second by his son Captain R. St V. Sherbrooke, V.C., D.S.O., R.N., who died in 1972. He won his V.C. and lost an eye in successfully holding off German attacks on a Russian-bound convoy off the North Cape in 1942. The tomb of an earlier Sherbrooke, who died in 1710, is curiously sited in a woodyard opposite the Green Dragon Inn. The most likely explanation for this oddity is that Robert Sherbrooke was a Quaker—once a flourishing sect in Oxton—and that this was the site of their Meeting House. The Sherbrookes were closely related to the Lowes of Oxton, one of whom, Robert, wrote *A General View of Agriculture in the County of Nottingham* in 1802. A later Lowe inherited the Oxton estate and took the name of Sherbrooke. One other feature of Oxton that may puzzle visitors is the State flag of Pennsylvania that hangs in the church. It was presented in 1951 in memory of 'Five Sons of Oxton' who sailed with William Penn in 1684 to found the state.

The relatively high ground in the Oxton-Farnsfield-Halam triangle is the richest in Nottinghamshire for pre-historic sites. Several hill-tops are crowned with Iron Age earthworks, but the land within these enclosures has yielded evidence of occupation in Bronze Age and even Neolithic times. Oldox (or Iverishagh), a mile north of Oxton, is one of the best preserved and most elaborately built. A mile or so farther north, Combs Farm Camp is an oval promontory fortress (best approached from Farnsfield, a mile or so north-east), standing on an ancient trackway running from Nottingham to Bawtry. Several of these hill-top sites were occupied in Roman times and later. An Anglo-Saxon burial place has been excavated near Oldox.

South of Oxton on the A6097, Lowdham is uninteresting, apart from the strange position of its church, outside the village on the north bank of the Cocker Beck, and a corn mill that has been cleverly converted into a private house without disturbing its water-wheel.

Who could resist following the Cocker Beck to Lambley Dumbles? The names are irresistible. Places are not always as lovely as they sound, but fortunately Lambley Dumbles, with the land rising quite sharply away from it on three sides, is decidedly pretty. Lambley village is rewarding too. It has one of the finest Perpendicular village churches in the county, 'all of a piece and of felicitous proportions', almost untouched from its building around 1450 through the generosity of Ralph, Lord Cromwell, who was born in the village about 1394 and became Lord High Treasurer of England. Besides the church he left two other splendid monuments, both outside the county: Wingfield Manor in Derbyshire and Tattershall Castle in Lincolnshire.

Gedling, south-west of Lambley, has another fine church, with a truly magnificent steeple that has dominated the landscape hereabouts since around 1300. In Gedling churchyard, separated by roughly the length of a cricket pitch, are the graves of those two great Nottinghamshire and England cricketers Arthur Shrewsbury and Alfred Shaw, of whom my grandfather used to speak in reverential tones. Great friends, they went into business together in Nottingham, making and selling cricket bats of high quality. But Gedling itself is now part of the Nottingham conurbation; it has a colliery, vast housing estates and other trappings of modern industrialised society. Only its church links it with the quieter world of Laxton, Maplebeck and Halam.

CHAPTER EIGHT

Along the Trent

The Trent is the third longest river in England, and for some 60 of its 180 miles it is a Nottinghamshire river. Unlike most rivers, it is not generally seen best from a boat, because—and here it has some affinity with the Severn—high banks along much of its course obstruct the view. So it is from those banks that you see the river at its best. And its best can be so good that you can see why Michael Drayton, some four centuries ago, called it the 'princely Trent'.

I must not overstate the case. It hardly competes with the middle reaches of either Thames or Severn for beauty; nor has it the bustle and excitement that you find lower down those rivers. It is, for the most part, a placid, unspectacular river offering what George Eliot called 'some charming, quiet landscapes', as well as occasional flashes of genuine beauty, which is something that could be said of the whole eastern side of the county.

Perhaps I am over-stressing the quietness. The Trent has always been a fairly busy commercial highway as far upstream as Nottingham. Over the three years 1970–72 an average of more than 500,000 tons of freight annually was transported along the river. But commercial vessels are now outnumbered by pleasure craft. A survey carried out in 1970 reported that the number of cabin cruisers moored at Trent Lock, close to Redhill tunnel, had increased from 50 to around 500 in a decade, while a few miles upstream there were now nearly 1,000 boats at moorings where ten years earlier there had been perhaps 25. In the same period the number of canoe clubs on the Trent and its tributaries had grown from two to 18, while the growth of rowing clubs was slowed only 'because existing facilities, buildings and equipment are being used to capacity.' And if sturgeon and salmon are now rare fish in a river they once frequented, there is certainly no scarcity of anglers. All this is to the good; a wide, slow-moving river needs life; the Trent now has this in abundance.

The most convenient way to write about the Trent is to go straight up the west bank and return on the east, but in practice the visitor may prefer to divide the river up into shorter stretches, using the bridges at Nottingham, Gunthorpe, Newark and Dunham. In this he has the advantage of earlier travellers, such as Byng and Defoe, who had to use one of numerous ferries to cross between there and the sea. With the building of toll-bridges at Dunham and Kelham in the nineteenth century, the importance of these ferries declined slightly, but most of them continued to operate until well into the motor-car age. Few are in use today, though many still appear on the map.

One of them gives its name to the riverside inn at Stoke Bardolph, the first village off the main Southwell road outside the Nottingham conurbation. The village cricket ground is unusually and attractively sited on the river bank close to the Nottingham County Sailing Club, and though most of the houses are modern there is a breezy atmosphere about the place that matches its jolly Shakespearean name.

The river takes a wide loop northward almost to the Southwell road at Burton Joyce, a growing, commuter village that straggles down from the Keuper ridge. Joyce, rather disappointingly, is simply a corruption of de Joriz, local landowners in medieval times when Simon de Montfort held the neighbouring riparian manor of Gunthorpe, a village that is seen to better advantage from the east bank. The wise driver will avoid the A6097 to Gunthorpe bridge and take the next turning to Caythorpe and Hoveringham.

Caythorpe is an attractive little place which has retained a few Georgian houses and a small framework knitters' workshop. Caythorpe Mill, a corn mill of 1749, has been cleverly converted into a private house with a pretty garden. Hoveringham Mill on the Dover Beck between Caythorpe and Hoveringham, was still grinding corn until about 1960 and its machinery is intact and usually available for inspection. It is best reached along a bridlepath from Hoveringham village, a mile away. The village itself lies about a mile back from the Trent, but there is an inn on the river bank looking out along one of the loveliest reaches. The east bank along here is well wooded and climbs steeply up to about 200 ft with the tower of Kneeton church superbly crowning the ridge called Trent Hills.

Needless to say, the lane that hugs the river bank between Caythorpe and Hoveringham—like the one at Stoke Bardolph—is crowded with traffic on a summer Sunday; the English being inveterate water-watchers. But on weekdays the riverside is quiet enough, though in the lanes you have to look out for heavy lorries carrying gravel from the quarries. Hoveringham is the centre of this important local industry. It is not one that adds beauty to the landscape while quarrying is in progress, but disused gravel pits can often be made attractive afterwards to bring pleasure to many people, like the Attenborough nature reserve (mentioned in Chapter Three), or the first national water sports centre at Holme Pierrepoint, of which more later. And it should be said that some of the most important archaeological finds locally have been made in gravel pits, or in the Trent itself, from which, incidentally, some 350,000 tons are dredged annually and shipped down river. On the whole, it seems that planners and gravelmen have reached a reasonable compromise along the Trent valley. Certainly, the pits at Hoveringham are fairly unobtrusive and the administrative buildings are quite neatly—if rather clinically—landscaped.

They stand by the road to Thurgarton station, which lies in the valley away from the village and is the best of several charming Victorian-Elizabethan stations on the Nottingham-Lincoln line. To get back to the river you have to join the Southwell road, briefly, before recrossing the railway at Bleasby and heading for Hazleford Ferry, where there is an inn called the Star and Garter, arguably the prettiest view on the whole river, and masses of people at weekends. On the east bank opposite the inn, Flintham Woods rise thickly and steeply from a stretch of water that reminds me of Cliveden Reach in miniature. Just below the inn and above Ladies Piece is a weir, and a lock to bypass it. Somewhere here, according to one tradition, Paulinus baptised his first converts from this area, though another theory places the first baptisms downstream at North Muskham. On a quiet day Hazleford Ferry is a marvellous place, best viewed from a boat, despite what I said earlier. I have forgotten who described this as 'one of the most pleasant stretches of river in the country', but I am with him wholeheartedly.

The river is straighter and the banks less woody at Fiskerton, but the village, peering over the high embankment, is one of the most attractive on the Trent. There is a quay, a malthouse, a crane, a slipway and a charming riverside inn called the Bromley Arms, kept, appropriately enough, by Mrs Tavner, who served me delicious sandwiches with my half pint in a bar overlooking the river. But it is not so much the individual buildings that you remember at Fiskerton; it is the general character of the place; especially those pantiles sparkling in the sun.

The River Greet comes down from Southwell to join the Trent halfway between Fiskerton and Rolleston. The old corn mill, later converted to a cotton mill, stands to the left of the road, but is now rather lost in modern mill buildings. Rolleston is another village of character, with several of those solid-looking red brick farmhouses that are a feature of Nottinghamshire. The church has an impressive tower and an interesting interior containing some Norman work, but the average visitor will probably be most attracted to the fragment of a Saxon cross built into the wall which has scratched on it the words '*Radulfus me fe*', ('Radulf made me'). It is one of the few surviving pieces of Saxon work in England that bears the signature of the craftsman who made it. Beyond the church is something perhaps even more surprising. The lane peters out, apparently in the fields, but there, quite unexpectedly, is a car park sign, which seems to have been left over from some agricultural show. But in fact you have reached what must surely be one of the most rural of National Hunt race-courses. If you have never heard of racing at Rolleston this is because the meetings there are known as Southwell Races. Originally they were run at Low Wongs, Southwell, some four miles away, to enter-tain pilgrims to the Minster at the Feast of Pentecost.

After depressing Staythorpe, dominated by a giant power station and its distressing wirescape, Averham provides several pleasant surprises. Most of them are well off the main road at the far end of the village (pronounced Ayram, by the way, which is surprising in itself), where Norman church and late-Georgian rectory cling together almost on the edge of a lovely reach of the Trent. The setting is beautiful; so are the buildings—especially the church with some herringbone masonry and many memorials of the Sutton family— but the biggest surprises are in the leafy rectory grounds. A Perpen-dicular aisle window from Southwell Minster built into a garden wall is unexpected enough; a live theatre in the garden is positively astonish-ing. It was started by a former rector, the Rev Cyril Walker, who had a taste for drama and a flair for painting scenery. That was in 1913. He died in 1941 and ten years later the theatre closed, apparently for the last time. But in 1961 it was revived by Mrs Valerie Baker and today

29. (opposite, above) *Balderton Church*

30. (below) *Thrumpton Hall, built 1607 but incorporating earlier work including a priest's hole*

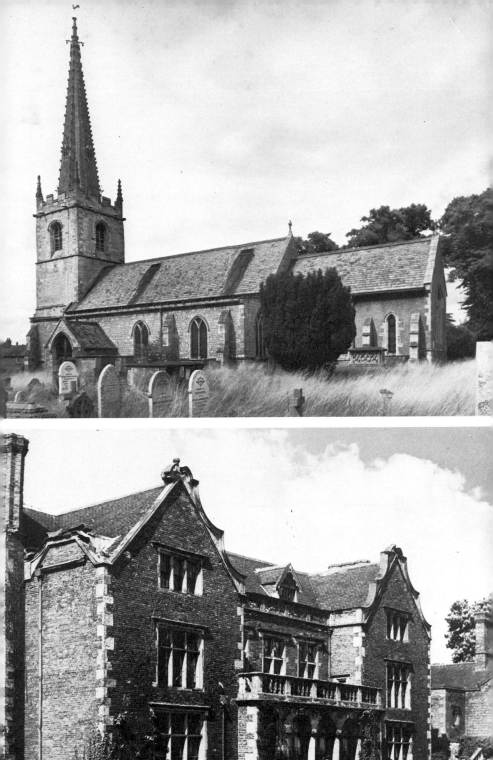

the Robin Hood Theatre is a well-established professional theatre, with a season that runs from February to late October.

At Averham Weir the waters of Trent divide. The main channel swings northward; the Cut, the navigation channel, follows the old course south and then east to Newark, where it is joined by the Devon (pronounced Deevon).

Following the west bank of the main stream, you come, along a short stretch of main road, to Kelham, dominated by the tall, spikey Anglican theological college, shortly to be closed. Impressive at a distance, it is less so at close range because of its unattractive brickwork and stone dressings. It was built by George Gilbert Scott (later Sir Gilbert) after fire had destroyed the old Kelham Hall, once the home of the Suttons, in 1857. Even that house was not the 'Kelum Hall' to which Charles I was taken by the Scottish Commissioners. That also was burnt down—half a century after the King's visit. Kelham's buildings seem to have been unlucky; the wooden predecessor of its present five-arch bridge over the Trent was cut in two by floating ice in the nineteenth-century.

If you can resist the temptation to turn over the bridge to Newark, you can leave the main road at the far end of Kelham and follow the river to South Muskham, the southernmost of a string of sizeable villages—North Muskham, Cromwell, Carlton-on-Trent and Sutton-on-Trent are the others—that have recently been liberated from the fuss, fumes and frenzy of the Great North Road. Indeed it was probably a second liberation for all but Cromwell, as in the other places the village centre lies just east of even the old A1. This is now an ideal road for the reluctant motorist, so wide, well-surfaced and quiet as to tempt you to press on, which would be a mistake, for these are pleasant, prosperous-looking riverside villages with splendidly-spired churches and more than a sprinkling of gracious houses of the eighteenth century and earlier.

Most of the churchyards offer good views of the river and all the churches are worth seeing. North Muskham is a favourite of mine. Who could resist the grinning gargoyles, the splendid chancel, or the rebus of the Bartons—a tun (or barrel) with a bar across—in one of the windows? John Barton, whom we shall meet again at Holme, on the opposite bank, built the north aisle—and presumably the magnificent clerestory—in the fifteenth century. But the Mering Chapel in

31. (opposite, above) *Colston Bassett. The market cross in National Trust property*

32. (below) *Willoughby on the Wolds*

Sutton-on-Trent church is the showpiece hereabouts. It dates from around 1525, and has pinnacles rising from its buttresses, panelled battlements, a superb oak screen, most delicately carved, and a Purbeck marble tomb, presumably of Sir William Mering.

Cromwell, which gave its name to the family we have already met at Lambley, had a Roman bridge whose pillars were uncovered in 1884. Today it has a weir, built in 1911 and rebuilt after severe flood damage in 1956–57. North of the lock that bypasses it, the river is tidal. Technically, it is the beginning of the 52 miles of estuary, incidentally, though one hates to mention the fact, the most polluted estuary in Britain.

Fortunately, there is little evidence of pollution as the river winds northward. Carlton-on-Trent, the first estuarine village is indeed particularly pleasant. Its once noted Bell Inn is now a farmhouse and it has a smithy, like the one at Gonalston, with a brick horse-shoe round the entrance embellished with another advertising rhyme. 'Quaint', we murmur admiringly of such primitive advertising; 'monstrous', we say of twentieth century slogans on buildings. Odd, is it not?

At Sutton-on-Trent, where the Great North Road swings away north-westward, a minor road heads due north for Dunham Bridge. But before we cross the Trent there are some small but rewarding villages to see on the west bank. A decade or so ago one would have used the adjective 'remote' to describe these low-lying settlements linked by lanes, but today they are dominated by giant power stations. There is one at High Marnham, so called because at 58 ft above sea level it stands 30 ft above its twin settlement Low Marnham. The church is at Low Marnham and is worth visiting, not least for the memorials to the Cartwright family and for a housekeeper of theirs, Mary Outram, who 'resigned her breath' in 1778 after 45 years' service at Marnham Hall, long since demolished. Her last master, William Cartwright, who led a campaign for the abolition of tips to servants, fathered four sons as talented as the Denisons, who, coincidentally, bought the Cartwrights' Ossington estate. The best known was Edmund, another ingenious clergyman, who invented the power-loom in 1787, but his brother John was an even more powerful figure locally. Having resigned his naval commission rather than fight against the American colonists, he joined the Nottinghamshire

Militia, and as Major Cartwright became a pioneer Radical reformer. As early as 1776 he published a pamphlet advocating electoral reforms that were to become the main planks in the Chartist platform some 60 years later. Another brother, George ('Labrador') wrote the first sociological study of the Eskimoes, and the fourth was a successful naval officer who once created a stir by handing his prize-money of £1,000 to his ship's company.

At Fledborough a viaduct of 43 stone arches and four iron ones carries the Sheffield-Lincoln railway line across the Trent. The church, exceptionally rich in fourteenth-century glass, had an eighteenth-century parson named Sweetapple who worked a profitable racket in instant marriages before Lord Hardwicke's Marriage Act of 1753 tightened up the laws.

North of the busy Sheffield-Lincoln road and railway, are the attractive Lanehams. Church Laneham has a good beach at low tide, and, inevitably, caravans. The church, on a wooded knoll overlooking the river, is almost entirely Norman including, possibly, the south door itself, as well as the unmistakable Norman doorway. Even an oak chest bound with iron and carved with three rosettes, and 14 plain benches are probably at least 700 years old. Much later—but still dating back more than three centuries—is the elaborate monument in the chancel to two Markhams, father and son. Father was reputedly 'the lion' referred to by Queen Elizabeth I in her rhyming couplet:

> *Gervase the Gentle, Stanhope the stout,*
> *Markham the Lion, and Sutton the lout.*

Rampton, a mile and half north of Laneham, is known for its criminal mental hospital, which in fact lies well outside the village to the west and looks more agreeable than one expects, but the principal attraction lies obscurely between the church and a farmyard. It is a magnificent Tudor gateway, 'an uncommonly lavish piece of Early Tudor decoration', says Pevsner, 'rising in three stepped stages and adorned with corbelled-out panels of terra-cotta with coats-of-arms'. It once led to the home of the de Ramptons, Eyres and Babingtons, now replaced by a Victorian mansion whose grounds are entered by a copy of the Tudor one that John Babington erected.

Farther north still, both the Levertons, South and North, are delightful. Both have good churches; the slim west tower at South

Leverton is almost wholly Norman, which is unusual in Nottinghamshire. Both have dovecotes, and attractive brickwork and Dutch gables from the seventeenth and eighteenth centuries, and indeed the two villages look as if they had been transported from the Netherlands. To complete this illusion, North Leverton has a windmill.

The North Leverton Subscription Mill, so called because its erection in 1813 was paid for by subscriptions from farmers in four neighbouring parishes, is the only windmill in the county still grinding corn. A three-storied tower mill built of brick and surmounted by a wooden ogee cap of the traditional East Midland type, it was rebuilt and its four sails were renewed between 1959–61 after lightning struck one of the sails. To meet the cost of around £3,000 the then newly-formed Friends of the Windmill and a non-profit-making Windmill Company, which had succeeded the Subscription Company in 1956, were assisted generously by the County Council and various other bodies. The mill is now open to the public.

Until the 1960s the windmill, and the magnificent 12-pinnacled church tower that so thoroughly earns its credit title in the village name of Sturton-le-Steeple, were the outstanding landmarks hereabouts; today they are dwarfed by the power stations at West Burton and Cottam. Not that these new industrial giants are too bad to look at; much thought has gone into making them fit acceptably into this curiously evocative landscape; on the whole, successfully. But the lost pre-eminence of 'Le-Steeple' is regrettable, especially as the body of the church was so damaged by fire in 1901 that it had to be rebuilt. Hodgson Fowler did a good job, using what was usable of the original material. The Norman bowl of the font came from the vanished church of West Burton. Several interesting monuments are of members of the Thornhaugh family, including a floorstone over the tomb of Sir Francis, the Cromwellian soldier who was killed at the Battle of Preston. Only fragments remain of their old home at Fenton, the birthplace of the Elizabethan sailor, Frobisher's friend Edward Fenton, who once had serious thoughts of proclaiming himself King of St Helena.

Sturton stands on a Roman road from Doncaster to Lincoln. Follow that road south-east and you come to *Segelocum* where the road forded the river to become Till Bridge Lane. Today the tiny village, in Sturton parish, is called Littleborough and there is a trunk telegraph cable alongside the ford that was visible in the 1933 drought. Littleborough is little indeed and it has a proportionately tiny aisleless Norman church with lots of herringbone masonry and odd pieces of Roman tiles. Archaeologists have turned up many Roman relics at Littleborough, but a sexton with a spade made the most dramatic discovery when, in 1860, he found a stone coffin containing the body of a young woman wearing a garment secured by a Roman brooch. On exposure to air the body crumbled to dust. *Segelocum's* dissolution was more gradual.

Trentside along here is a good place to view the aegir. This is the tidal bore, less famous perhaps than those on the Severn or the Seine, but quite impressive. What happens is that the incoming spring tide (which occurs fortnightly and not just in the spring) is squeezed by converging banks as it meets a down flowing current. The result is a hissing wall of water that rises to six feet at equinoctial springs.

You can cross the Trent by Gainsborough Bridge, but as this involves driving through a large area of Lincolnshire before returning to Nottinghamshire, the fairer proposition is to go southward to Dunham, a reasonably attractive village with a fine church tower enriched high up by superb Perpendicular windows. Dunham Bridge, unfortunately, is a narrow, unattractive, iron structure alongside an even narrower and uglier aqueduct carrying an iron water pipe across the river. Built in 1832 to replace a ferry, the bridge is a source of irritation to the million or more motorists a year who lose time and money in paying toll charges, and of delight to the shareholders of the Dunham Bridge Company who benefit by more than £85,000 annually. Cyclists fare better; like pedestrians they cross free.

The east side of the bridge is in Lincolnshire, but Nottinghamshire is quickly regained south of the A57, where a curious tongue of flat, gravelly land protrudes into Lincolnshire, and seems to belong in atmosphere to that county but in fact forms the major part of the Newark Rural District, where 16,000 people live in an area of 65 square miles. That is two and a half acres per person. Over most of England you would have to go back to the Middle Ages to find parallel figures.

There are few major 'tourist attractions' in this remote countryside of tiny, red-roofed villages and scattered farmhouses. Broadholme, all but surrounded by Lincolnshire, has lost almost all trace of its nunnery of Premonstratensian Canonesses. One of them, Margaret Everingham, was abducted in 1349 by a local parson and two Franciscan friars; an unlikely-sounding, exciting story which unfortunately has no discoverable ending, except that the parson continued to hold his living for many years after the incident.

A queen died at Harby, the next village south. She was Eleanor of Castile, wife of Edward I. Taken ill in the manor house, she died there on 27 November 1290. Her body was taken to Lincoln to be embalmed and then conveyed to London by a route later to be marked by Eleanor crosses on the order of her husband, who 'loved her tenderly', as he said in a letter to the Abbot of Cluny, 'and I do not cease to love her now she is dead'. But there is not much to remember her by at Harby; just an inscription on the altar steps and traces of the moat of the manor house.

Nearer to the Trent, the villages tend to pair off; North and South Clifton, with the church standing in splendidly impartial isolation midway between them, the Scarles and the Collinghams, though North Scarle is actually in Lincolnshire. All are well worth exploring for their fine churches and many interesting houses. The Collinghams merge into one long linear village on the east bank of the old course of the Trent—now called The Fleet. The present course of the Trent now runs a mile away, but in 1795 it flooded the village to a depth of five feet, according to a plaque on the base of the old village cross near the church, and a second flood in 1875 was only slightly lower. In 1972 Collingham achieved a pleasanter kind of fame when its cricket team reached the semi-final of the national John Haig Cup for village clubs–and repeated the performance in 1973.

The Trent has always been a restless river, changing its course in places many times over the centuries. The alteration west of Collingham took place around 1600. The Fleet leaves the present course at Besthorpe, where there is a wharf for loading gravel, and maroons the small village of Holme virtually on an island; an extremely interesting island. On no account miss Holme Church. Externally, with its red pantile roof and low broach spire. it looks picturesque but unremarkable. Internally, however, it is a little gem of an early Tudor church, beautifully light and airy. Its most notable feature is the two-tier monument to John Barton and his wife, with two finely carved effigies on the upper tier and a rotting corpse below. John Barton, whom we have already met at North Muskham, died in 1491, shortly after he had rebuilt the church with some of his profits from the wool trade with France. In a window of his house at Holme, now a farmhouse, he inscribed the much quoted couplet:

I thank God and ever shall
It's the sheepe hath payed for all.

The window has not survived, unfortunately, but in the east window of the church he so superbly rebuilt are fragments of ancient glass skilfully pieced together in his memory. The two-storeyed south porch was part of his rebuilding. Of the seven carved shields over the door one is of the Staple of Calais with sheep below. The upper room of the porch is called Nanny Scott's Chamber after an old lady who shut herself off with several weeks' rations to dodge the plague that was raging in the neighbourhood, apparently in 1665.

A lane going south from Holme crosses The Fleet in the agreeable and prosperous-looking village of Winthorpe, where the county agricultural show is held on the first weekend in May on a permanent showground sited in an angle formed by the Fosse Way and the A1(T). North-east of Winthorpe, on the Fosse Way (A46) is the site of the Roman posting station of *Crococalana*, which is now called Brough, but as there is nothing to see except a tiny mid-Victorian church and a remarkably straight stretch of main road it is more sensible to follow the Fosse Way in the opposite direction into Newark.

Newark-on-Trent is a splendid town. Every visitor over the centuries seems to have agreed on that. Even the pungent William Cobbett called it 'a very fine town'. John Wesley said it was one of the most elegant towns in England. More recently the Council for British Archaeology has listed it among the best 50 towns in the country. Certainly few towns of its size (around 25,000 inhabitants) have retained so well and so unselfconsciously their medieval street pattern and so many good old buildings.

That lack of selfconsciousness which accounts for so much of its charm has also nearly been its undoing. The point is that Newark, like King's Lynn until recently, has never really regarded itself as a tourist attraction. As a route-town and an agricultural centre, with the sort of industries that have their origins in agriculture, it has long been accustomed to overnight visitors heading elsewhere rather than those who have come to see Newark for its own sake. In the motor car age it has been far too full of traffic to encourage long-term tourists. This is still true even though it has shrugged off the Great North Road traffic, which now crosses the Trent at Winthorpe by one of those excellent modern bridges that may come to be regarded as this century's major contribution to architecture. Because of these factors, coupled with its moderate size and its comparative distance from other tourist centres—Lincoln apart—Newark has neither attracted the big property developers nor inspired local property owners to renovate their own buildings. As a result few buildings have been demolished unnecessarily; a great many need repair. Out of a hundred buildings in the town centre, that in 1968 became one of the first conservation areas, all but 17 needed attention.

This fact emerged from a county council survey that has led to the introduction of the Newark Town Scheme, an enlightened five-year plan which should be completed in 1978. Under this scheme £120,000 will be available for the town's buildings, half supplied by the property owners, one-third by the Department of the Environment, £20,000 by the county council and £10,000 by the town council. But there is more to this town scheme than just making money available. The county planners are keeping an observant eye on such details as replacing slates with pantiles where there is evidence that pantiles were used before the railway age made slates the cheaper materials, and using timber of the same type and finish as the original.

At the same time the county planning department and town council are tidying up the riverside area around the castle and wharf. There is to be shopping development; better still, a relief road should clear the town of its through traffic before 1980. The result should be a well-maintained historic town; good to live in and to visit.

Or rather, an even better place, for Newark today, as I have already said, is admirable. Dominated by its ruined castle and its parish church, it has lying between them an area of fine buildings of varying ages and a market place that 'look'd fine' to Celia Fiennes and has more recently been described as 'the best in England'.

But we had better start with the castle, because it is where most tourists are likely to start and also because it was the residence of the lords of the manor for the best part of four centuries. They were successive Bishops of Lincoln. It was Bishop Alexander who rather tactlessly built the castle about 1129 and was subsequently sent to prison by Stephen, who was sensitive about military fortifications. It remained Crown property until 1216, the year in which King John on that doubly unfortunate journey in which he lost his jewels in the Wash, was taken ill at Swineshead Abbey, near Sleaford, and was moved to Newark Castle where he died a few days later. The castle was returned to the Bishops of Lincoln and remained theirs until Bishop Rands sold the Manor of Newark in 1547 to the Crown. Almost a century later, at the end of the Civil war, the castle was slighted. Newark Corporation bought the remains in 1889 and laid out the pleasant gardens between them and the public library.

All that survives is the north gateway and part of the west wall with its towers. The gateway, built on three large arches, is by far the most interesting portion. Indeed, Pevsner calls it 'the biggest and most elaborate of its period [1170–75] in England'. The upper portion was divided into two parts, reached by the same spiral staircase: the northern portion, on two floors, the private apartments of the Bishop or the Governor of the castle, the southern portion the chapel. Of the rest, there is a twelfth-century crypt, a pleasing oriel window with the coat-of-arms of Thomas Scot, who became Bishop of Lincoln in 1471 and subsequently Archbishop of York, an interesting view across the canalized arm of the Trent, and a host of memories of Newark's heroic resistance in the Civil War.

The town was a Royalist stronghold throughout the war. Three times it was besieged; each time it held out. Surrender came only when the King, then at Kelham, ordered it on 9 May 1646. Then the garrison were allowed to march out with full military honours.

During those years the King spent much time at the castle, but it was at the Governor's House, a half-timbered late-sixteenth century building still standing in Stodman Street, that he had the furious row with Prince Rupert, fully described by Clarendon, that ended in the Prince losing his post as General and Sir Richard Willis his as Governor of Newark.

Only a few paces from the Governor's House is that wonderful market place which Pevsner understandably found a 'joy to examine', dominated by the former White Hart Inn, 'one of the paramount examples of fourteenth century timber-framed domestic architecture in England'. Below its overhanging first and second storeys it has 24 closely placed vertical posts adorned by plaster figures of angels and saints; above is the inevitable pantile roof. It is one of the finest inn fronts in England. And only a few yards away are two other handsome inns: the Saracen's Head and the Clinton Arms. Both stand on piazzas with Tuscan columns; both appear to date from the eighteenth century, but the history of the Saracen's Head can be traced back further. Sir Walter Scott often stopped there and had Jeanie Deans sleep there in the *Heart of Midlothian*. Gladstone preferred the Clinton Arms. He stayed there when winning his first election in 1832 and subsequently during his 14 years as Member for Newark. Byron used the same inn—then called the Kingston Arms—when his *Hours of Idleness* (1806) and *Fugitive Pieces* (1808) were being printed by John Ridge on the corner of this superb square that Byng (another patron of the Kingston) called 'a very shewy, grand place'.

All Newark must have been 'shewy' when Byng saw it in 1789, for many of its houses were built or rebuilt just before then. The most notable is John Carr's Town Hall, also in the Market Place, in Mansfield stone. From other periods are good Tudor buildings in Kirkgate and a delightfully cheery piece of Victoriana opposite the castle. This is the Ossington Coffee Palace, designed by Ernest George and Peto with a row of six oriel windows on the first floor, and tall chimneys above, and no expense spared by Lady Ossington (Speaker Denison's widow) in her 'earnest desire to promote the cause of temperance'. She lost. The Coffee Palace now houses the Ministry of Social Security.

But I have left till last Newark's finest building. The church of St Mary Magdalen is the best town church in Nottinghamshire and, as Pevsner conservatively puts it, 'among the two or three dozen grandest parish churches in England'. Like St Mary's, Nottingham, it is essentially a Perpendicular building, mainly of the fifteenth century, though there is some earlier work, including the west tower and its slender fourteenth-century spire that dominates this part of the valley. Equally essentially, it is a monument to the wealth of the medieval wool merchants. There are two obvious clues to that. One is the brass to Alan Fleming, a Newark merchant, presumably of Flemish origin, who died in 1373. It is one of the four largest brasses of Flemish work in England. The other clue is another Mering Chapel, only slightly less distinguished than that at Sutton-on-Trent. It was founded by Thomas Mering, who in his will of 1500 instructed his executors to sell his 'clipped wole and all his floke of shepe' to pay for it. This is on the north side of the high altar. On the opposite side is a rather similar Markham Chapel of roughly the same date, with two fairly crude paintings of the 'Dance of Death'. Contemporary with the chapels are the rood screen and the choir stalls with 26 misericords. The spacious, airy transepts, lit by magnificent windows, are places to linger in and to contemplate a church whose whole is even more splendid than its parts.

Within two miles of Beaumond Cross, a slender shaft in the town centre of unknown date and purpose, are two other fine churches. Balderton, now virtually a suburb, has a fine steeple and an even finer Norman doorway with an inner order of primitive beakheads along the jambs and arch. In a niche above the doorway is a slightly later figure of the Virigin of the Annunciation. Hawton is a village church of exceptional quality. Its prominent fifteenth-century tower of Ancaster limestone stands out invitingly across the valley. The invitation should be accepted. The chancel alone is worth going well out of your way to see. Built by Sir Robert de Compton, who died in 1330, it is spacious, lit by a correspondingly large seven-light east window and enriched by exquisite carving that, despite some mutilation in the Commonwealth period, still displays the excellence of the York Guild of Masons. The founder's tomb, the outstandingly good double piscina and tripartite sedilia all demand attention, but the greatest glory of this superb chancel is the Easter sepulchre.

Elsewhere in the county, only fragments of Easter sepulchres survived the mid-seventeenth century wave of puritan vandalism. This one somehow escaped fairly lightly. It is in three richly carved parts. In the lowest portion four Roman soldiers crouch, apparently asleep. In the middle and largest part, the headless figure of Christ is seen rising from the grave. To the left is the niche in which the sacrament was placed on Good Friday to be guarded until dawn on Easter Sunday, when it would be brought out and placed on the altar, thus symbolising the Burial and Resurrection of Christ. The Ascension is represented in the upper portion.

Just west of Hawton Church an earthwork by the River Devon marks the outer south-western defences of Newark in the Civil War.

A better known defensive earthwork erected for the same purpose is the 'Queen's Sconce', which lies closer to Newark just east of the Fosse Way.

For the first few miles out of Newark towards Nottingham this is a disquietingly straight and narrow road on which the quick and the dead are all too often synonymous. You can take temporary refuge in Farndon, which has some good Georgian houses, an avenue of limes leading to a much restored church that still has some Norman herringbone masonry, the headquarters of the Trent Sailing Club, and a boat-repair yard, but there is no major escape route on the river side of the Roman road before the Kneeton turning. Before that though, a lane opposite the Pauncefote Arms meanders through the meadows for a mile, ending unexpectedly with a charming view of Fiskerton, 70 yards away across the Trent.

The inn takes its name from former owners of Stoke Hall, descendants of Abel Smith, the Nottingham banker, who bought the estate in 1750. Sir Julian Paunceforte, later Lord Pauncefote—(1828–1902) became the first ambassador to the United States, not just the first British ambassador, but, astonishingly, the first representative of any nation to hold that title, because until 1893 the States did not send ambassadors abroad. When Congress decided they should Pauncefote, who had already been Minister in Washington for four years, immediately became Ambassador. When he died in harness, the body of this 'damn good fellow', as Teddy Roosevelt described him, was sent back to England for burial in the churchyard at East Stoke, close to the Hall.

But East Stoke is better known as the site of one of the bloodiest battles ever fought in England. It took place on 16 June, 1487, two years after the Battle of Bosworth. The Yorkists, led by the Earl of Lincoln and Viscount Lovel, had with them the pretender Lambert Simnel, as they marched to seize Newark, 'the key to the north'. But around the crossroads at East Stoke they met the army of Henry VII that had moved out from Nottingham. The Yorkists were routed; part of their army driven back to the Trent.

Battles are not easy to reconstruct on the ground without a detailed account and a large-scale map. I have never been able to make much of this one. But there are a few significant local names; Deadman's Field, for instance, and Red Gutter, which is supposed to have run with blood but is more likely to have taken its name from the colour of the soil.

Just beyond the southern edge of the battlefield a deserted chapel stands in a field on the outskirts of Elston. The early eighteenth century stone-built Elston Hall nurtured yet another of those large and remarkably talented families; the Darwins. Ann Darwin founded, in 1744, the almshouses opposite the church, where there are other Darwin monuments, but not one of the most eminent of the Elston branch; that admirable all-rounder, Erasmus Darwin (1731–1802).

This master of all trades—scientist, inventor, reformer, physician, poet, philosopher and prophet, among other things—might have become as famous as his grandson Charles if he had been content to specialize. But his inquiring mind tilled many fields of knowledge, ranging far beyond the eighteenth century. He forecast the coming of submarines, motor cars and aeroplanes—and indeed—invented a gunpowder-operated flying machine. He drew up workable plans for canal locks, sewage disposal and carriage suspension, and invented a typewriter and a speaking machine. He even invented a speaking robot, but it proved somewhat inarticulate and never managed to say more than 'papa' and 'mama'. All this activity he crammed into what spare time was available from a flourishing medical practice based on Lichfield, after he left Nottingham at 25, that took him all over the Midlands and beyond, despite the apparent handicap of a stutter and a lack of either good looks or a smooth bedside manner. Such a man might have seemed predestined to bachelordom, but in fact Erasmus Darwin enjoyed two happy marriages and adroitly side-stepped what might have been a less happy one with the determined poetesss Anna Seward. He was a man who combined common sense with his idealism, ability and enormous zest for life.

Syerston, once the scene of a brisk Civil War skirmish, is now dominated by an airfield, and the Fosse Way is littered with those road signs that have you wondering just how you avoid low-flying aircraft. Beyond the airfield the land rises gently to Trent Hills that reach 250 ft south of Kneeton, a quiet, attractive village with a fine view down into the Trent valley from the over-restored church. An old tower mill, now without sails, is part of the Old Mill Farm smallholdings estate run by the county council.

The next village, East Bridgford, is larger, beautifully wooded and altogether decidedly comely, though its most interesting features are invisible underground. These are the foundations of a cruciform

Saxon church, and, more important, the traces of the Roman village station of *Margidunum*, excavated between the wars by Dr Felix Oswald. The Old Hall was the home of the Hacker family, strongly Royalist in the Civil War except for Colonel Francis Hacker, to whom the death warrant of Charles I was delivered. He conducted the king to the scaffold at Whitehall, and some 16 years later, he was led himself to another at Tyburn.

A steep, wooded hill leads down to the river at Gunthorpe Bridge, a between-wars product that replaced the iron toll bridge of 1875. From the east bank there is a good view of Gunthorpe Green and Gunthorpe Lock, the second lock below Nottingham.

A pleasant riverside lane leads on to Shelford, a delectable red-roofed village standing at the open end of a great horseshoe bend of of the Trent. An atavistic sense of shame kept me out of the church 'so ruthlessly restored by the callous Mr Christian that little remains for enjoyment', despite the invitation of a handsome tower and the promise of a Chantrey wall monument and some Stanhope monuments. The Stanhopes, Earls of Chesterfield, acquired the small Austin Priory at the Dissolution and built on the site the manor house which Philip Stanhope garrisoned for Charles I in the Civil War with 200 men who conducted an effective guerrilla campaign against the Parliamentary forces in the Trent Valley until, in October 1645, they were overwhelmed and almost annihilated. The house was burnt down, but was rebuilt in 1676. A later Philip Stanhope was the fourth Earl of Chesterfield, that reluctant patron of Dr Johnson and author of those famous letters to a son who apparently failed to profit from them, though his widow subsequently did by publishing them, to the annoyance of her father-in-law. The fourth Earl's bones lie at Shelford, having earlier been buried in London.

Malkin Hill is a watershed (200 ft up) separating rural Shelford from suburban Radcliffe-on-Trent. But all is not quite lost at Radcliffe. There are a few Georgian buildings and an attractive memorial garden on the red cliff, high above the river, that gave the village its name.

The lane that appears on the map to link Radcliffe with Holme Pierrepont turns out to be a ferociously crated, soggy track suitable only for those who sight-see by tank. Avoid it by using a short stretch of the Grantham road (A52). But do not miss Holme Pierrepont, church and Hall, standing together, isolated from the village, beyond that ineffable lane. The mansion has changed greatly since the sharp-eyed Celia Fiennes admired its distant prospect from Nottingham Castle, but some of the windows at least are unchanged. The crenellations and stucco appeared when the house was enlarged and romanticized in 1790. A slightly later owner, with a more practical approach, demolished part of the house and restored the rest. The owners were the Pierrepont family, Earls and Dukes of Kingston, whom we have already met at Thoresby. They are almost innumerably and most interestingly commemorated in the church, several of them on fine alabaster tomb-chests. But two of the best memorials are not to Pierreponts. A sculpture by Flaxman of a woman reading a book is in memory of William Saltren, who skated on thin ice on Thoresby Lake in 1811, and a tablet on a pillar, so good that Pevsner is inclined to attribute it to Grinling Gibbons, recalls the almost forgotten Restoration poet John Oldham (1653–1683), a protégé of the Earl of Kingston. Apart from the monuments, the most striking feature of an architecturally curious mixture of the fourteenth and seventeenth centuries is the south porch with its Tuscan columns and massive cornice.

But it is not for ecclesiastical architecture or antiquarian attractions that Holme Pierrepont has now become nationally—even internationally—important. What has happened is that Nottinghamshire County Council's Planning Department have turned two disused gravel pits, covering 225 acres, into a multi-purpose water sports centre and country park, the first of its kind in Britain with facilities up to international standard. Its main course of 2,000 metres for rowing and canoeing came into use in August 1972, though some of its other facilities, such as the separate water-ski lagoon, were not ready for use until the following year. Now this rural retreat within five miles of the centre of Nottingham is equipped to deal with every form of water sport from sailing to angling and underwater swimming, and it is obviously destined to become an international centre for rowing.

Venturesome travellers willing to endure the discomforts of driving through the southern outskirts of Nottingham will be amply rewarded by some pleasant villages along the Trent to the south-west. Clifton, which earlier writers rated amongst the most beautiful in the county, has been all but engulfed by Nottingham, but has managed to retain some of the character of a village. The early-eighteenth century brick dovecote on the spacious green is the largest in the county, with 2,300 nesting places. Clifton Grove, where Paul Morel and Clare Dawes spent a delightful afternoon in *Sons and Lovers*, remains one of the finest of Trentside walks. Clifton Hall is now a school. For seven centuries it was the home of the Clifton family, whose monuments enrich the fine cruciform parish church. Among them is a bust of Sir Gervase (died 1666), who had, consecutively, seven wives, the first three of whom are commemorated in a monument of 1631.

From Clifton, a fast new road runs down to the M1 near Kegworth, just across the Leicestershire border, bypassing such villages as Barton-in-Fabis and Thrumpton. Barton-in-Fabis (which sounds more elegant if less descriptive than the earlier, plain English, Barton-in-the-Beans) is a charming place at an ancient ferry point that may have been used by the Romans, as there is a villa site nearby. The fourteenth-century chancel of the church, dedicated to the mythological St George, has an unusually tall and narrow chancel arch and contains fine alabaster monuments to Sacheverells (who became allied by marriage to the Sitwells), and some good incised signed gravestones of the eighteenth and nineteenth centuries.

Thrumpton is what eighteenth-century topographers would have called a 'neat' village. It is an attractively leafy place, bearing unmistakable evidence of centuries of benevolent squirearchal rule from Thrumpton Hall, home of the Hon. George Fitzroy Seymour (pronounced Seamer), which is open to parties of 20 or more by prior arrangement. The present house basically dates from 1607, but incorporates parts of a much earlier one, and there were substantial alterations and additions in the 1660s and 1820s. A priest's hole at the foot of a secret staircase built into the thickness of a chimney breast survives from the earliest house and was used by the then owners—the Roman Catholic Powdrill family—to conceal Father Garnett, one of the leading figures in the Gunpowder Plot of 1605. Because of their recusancy, the Powdrills had Thrumpton confiscated, but their successors, the Pigots, lost it some 90 years later because of the lavishness of their rebuilding in the reign of Charles II, of which the magnificence of the cantilevered staircase, richly carved on both sides and climbing to the top of the house, is acceptable evidence. The second

33. (opposite) *Bingham, in the Vale of Belvoir*

Gervase Pigot was forced to mortgage the estate, and in 1694 John Emerton foreclosed it and took possession. Thrumpton has descended from him ever since, but never directly from father to son. Perhaps its most remarkable owner was Lucy Emerton Westcomb, who subsequently married the eighth Lord Byron. She ruled her village, as Queen Victoria currently ruled England, for 68 years until her death aged 88 in 1912, inspiring both awe and affection and building up what was said to be the finest choir in the Southwell diocese by employing on her estate only good singers. It was her predecessor who insisted that Redhill tunnel, which bores under part of the park, should have entrances that as nearly as possible matched his entrance lodges, and was negotiating with the Midland Counties Railway an agreement that trains should stop in the park to pick up or set down members of his household at the time of his death in 1838.

The Trent ceases to be a Nottinghamshire river beyond Redhill, but the county extends southward along the east bank of its tributary the Soar almost into Loughborough. The five Soar villages are all attractive, even Ratcliffe-on-Soar, despite the dominance of a huge, but by no means oppressively ugly, power station, that certainly does not obscure the charm of the thirteenth-century church tower and only slightly later broach spire. If, inside the church, you have the feeling of having been there before it will be because of another batch of Sacheverell tombs, all in alabaster and possibly from the same workshop as those at Barton. A little gem of a church this, with a chancel longer than its nave and lit by a fine east window, but showing signs that it needs a lot more money for maintenance than a parish of its size—even though it is growing a little—can hope to raise. But this is a national problem.

It is not a problem that seems to arise at Kingston-on-Soar, a mile away down a road that marches under the lee of a railway embankment before suddenly darting under it into a greener, trim, slightly prim, estate village grouped round a triangular tree-lined green. The church, less than a century old, is tidy, dark and would be dull if it were not for the Babington Chantry, the finest chantry chapel in the county. Dating from about 1544, it must also be one of the last. It has been moved from its original position and lost most of its tomb-chest, but retained its pillared canopy, the richness of its carving and battlemented and pinnacled upperwork.

34. *Alabaster tomb of Lord Scrope and his wife, Philadelphia, with their son, Emanuel, kneeling at their feet, in Langar Church*

Whereas Kingston village is compact, its southern neighbour, Sutton Bonington, has immense length and no breadth, its shape being dictated by sharply rising ground on one side and the flood plain of the Soar on the other. That this sprawling village pleases is a tribute to the excellence of much of its housing, some of it half-timbered. There is one cruck cottage of great age, and nearby is one with jettied upper storey and herringbone work above a ground floor of Charnwood Forest stone from over the Leicestershire border. Originally, Sutton and Bonington were separate villages, which explains the two churches. St Michael's, the church of Bonington, is the larger. It has a fourteenth-century font with projections for book, salt and candle, and a long sloping graveyard which ends unexpectedly on the edge of a deep railway cutting, like a long open grave, from which the whine of diesel trains echoes eerily. All in all, an interesting village, enriched now by Nottingham University's Department of Agriculture, but it is a pity that the ribbon building that started so long ago should continue; there should surely be a limit.

Normanton-on-Soar bears a family likeness to Sutton Bonington, but its sprawl is less pronounced and its proportion of charming houses even higher. If there is a more beautiful post office than this black and white half-timbered little house with its thatched roof, I have yet to see it. And there are not many churches as close to a river as this one. Any experienced sailor from the Soar Boat Club, whose headquarters are nearby, could surely reach the south porch with a heaving-line.

The last of the Nottinghamshire villages in the Soar valley, a breezy stretch of wide skies, large farms and deep red soil, is Stanford-on-Soar, a pleasing estate village of 1839 built on a series of alarming bends leading to an ugly railway viaduct at the end of the village. Stanford Hall was the home of that cricket-loving tycoon, Sir Julian Cahn, and is now a residential Co-operative College. But that is two miles out of Stanford on the edge of the Wolds.

CHAPTER NINE

The Vale and the Wolds

The Wolds, a northern extension of the Leicestershire Wolds, stretch from the county boundary almost to the southern outskirts of Nottingham. Eastward, again reaching to the boundary, is the fertile Vale of Belvoir. On the map, the Fosse Way neatly divides the two areas, running almost along the edge of the Wolds from near East Bridgford southward, until it leaves the county. This is the Fosse at its best. After Saxondale crossroads it sheds much of its traffic and becomes an attractive, reasonably speedy drive, often through well-wooded country. But, being a Roman Road, it passes through not a single village between East Stoke and the county boundary, and its thick covering of greenery impedes any views across the Vale.

To get the most dramatic view, the best thing to do is drive out from Nottingham to Cotgrave, and then take the lane from near the church, signposted Owthorpe. Have a look first, though, at Cotgrave. It is almost a second Calverton, but more compact. A much-photographed church spire rises above elms and limes in the centre of an old agricultural village on to which has been grafted a new colliery village to serve the only coal mine in Nottinghamshire south of the Trent. Cotgrave's earlier holes in the ground were marl-pits from which came the dressing for cricket pitches as smooth as the proverbial shirt-front. They were certainly much less noticeable than the new mine that started production in 1964 and now sends up one million tons of coal a year.

But to get that view you must climb steeply up Wolds Hill out of Cotgrave and cross the Fosse Way at an awkward angle near Borders Wood. Then, almost at once, you are at the summit of Owthorpe Hill, which is little more than 250 ft, but seems three times that because, as Firth wrote: 'It is a quick fall, which affords as lovely a view of the Vale of Belvoir across to the Belvoir Heights as you will find for all your searching, and there is no richer or greener valley in the whole of England. And here, just at your feet, quietly tucked away in the shelter of the hill is the little village of Owthorpe. Today it is nothing but a sequestered hamlet of a few farms and cottages, with a church so small and unassuming that it can easily be missed.'

That was written in 1916, but not a word of it needs to be amended nearly 60 years later. It still 'looks a sleepy hollow which has never known disturbance', as indeed do most of the Vale villages. To get to Owthorpe church you have to open a field gate and walk across close-cropped turf for a couple of hundred yards; and it would be well worth a much longer and less pleasant walk. Like many other Vale churches, it has been reduced in size. The alterations here were made in 1705 and the church is basically of that period, but with some features of the old one—such as the timber screen, Jacobean pulpit above a reading desk, and the altar rails—that blend beautifully with the newer, in a small aisleless building whose charm has been enhanced by the bright blue and white of its interior walls.

Historically, the most interesting survival from the earlier church is the monument to Colonel John Hutchinson, the Civil War defender of Nottingham Castle. Having survived the war and, though his name was on the king's death warrant, the Restoration, 'he died', the inscription on his monument tells us, 'at Sandowne Castle in Kent, after 11 months harsh and strict imprisonment—without crime or accusation. . . .' This seems to be literally true. He was living quietly at his Owthorpe home (long since demolished), engaged in nothing more sinister than the planting of trees when he was arrested. He spent six months in the Tower of London (where, ironically, his wife Lucy, was born when her father, Sir Allen Apsley, was its governor) before being moved to even less salubrious quarters at Dover, Deal and finally to Sandown, where he died in September 1664, and from where the devoted Lucy saw to it that 'he was brought home with honour' for burial at Owthorpe.

The man responsible for Hutchinson's arrest 'was a light-headed, debauched young knight living in the next town', a certain Sir Francis Golding of Colston Bassett. Lucy Hutchinson may have been strictly correct in calling Colston Bassett a town, for it received the grant of a weekly market—and a thrice-yearly fair—in 1257 and still has its market cross to prove it. But today it is urbane rather than urban.

Like its neighbour, it has probably declined in size, but whereas Owthorpe wears a slight air of decay, Colston Bassett looks sleek, prosperous and uncommonly handsome. The Bassetts, up to the end of the fourteenth century, and successive squires since—including the Goldings—have done all but one of the right things with their domain, including planting the right trees in the right places at the right time so that they are superb today. The only mistake was to unroof the old church in 1892 and replace it with a townish Gothic revival church in memory of the reigning squire's wife and son. Admittedly it is nearer the village centre, but it is a pity that the older building was left to crumble away in a far corner of the park. One of the best buildings at Colston Bassett, as at Normanton-on-Soar, is the post office, which is featured on one of those excellent illustrated posters that advertise the Post Office corporation. Immediately opposite is a pleasant pub whose licensee is justly proud of his roses, and between the buildings stands the market cross which in 1933 became the National Trust's first property in Nottinghamshire, a somewhat bizarre choice, for though its site is old and its base may date from the fifteenth century, the incongruous classical column that now serves as a shaft was put there as late as 1831 to commemorate the coronation of William IV.

That Cropwell Bishop, the next village to the north, has reversed the general Vale trend of declining populations, is partly due to the gypsum bed underlying the parish, which with just over 1,000 inhabitants is now one of the largest in the area. The gypsum is processed in a sizeable works alongside the long-abandoned Grantham Canal south of the village, to which it is linked by undistinguished modern housing, though the village centre has retained its rural character. Its slightly smaller neighbour, Cropwell Butler, has a pleasant green around which some of the older houses have been modernized admirably, though a modern garage with a thatched roof strikes a slightly anachronistic note. Both the Cropwells tend to straggle, but Tythby, to the east, is strikingly compact, as indeed is its church, worth visiting for its Georgian furnishings. One does not have to be particularly imaginative to picture Parson Adams preaching from the two-decker pulpit in front of the high chancel rail to Squire Allworthy in his private pew and the rest of the congregation in strict order of status in their box pews.

Beyond Tythby a road runs northward over empty country to Bingham, where history seems to move in circles. A market town in

Edward II's reign and the headquarters of Bingham Hundred it gradually declined to village status and lost its market, if not its market place and steeple-roofed butter cross. Now the unofficial capital of the Vale, it is growing again and is destined by the planners to reach an eventual 30,000 population. So far, the new development has not entirely obliterated the old-world atmosphere and indeed the careful blending of old and new in the market place earned a 1962 Civic Trust Award. The church has a good broach spire, a portrait of Lily Langtry on the chancel screen and the distinction of having had three successive seventeenth-century rectors who became bishops. Lily Langtry is there because she, a clergyman's daughter, often stayed at Bingham Rectory and the artist, Frank Miles, was the rector's son. Of the local rectors who made good, the first, Abbot, was Archbishop of Canterbury from 1611 to 1633. He is now chiefly remembered for inadvertently killing a keeper, whom he mistook for a deer, during a hunting trip. Another was Wren, father of Sir Christopher. A later rector was Robert Lowe, father of the first Viscount Sherbrooke whom we have already met at Oxton. The Rev Robert Lowe was a hunting and shooting parson with an interest in poor law reform. His 'well-disciplined workhouse at Bingham' was held up as a model in its time, and though he seems to have been as hard on vagrants as on foxes and partridges, he was immensely popular in his parish.

The Vale has long been renowned as good hunting country, but Bingham can now offer excellent facilities for a much wider variety of sports. When Bingham Sports Centre opened in April 1969, it was the first of its type in the country. On five days a week it is used in working hours by a comprehensive school and in the evenings, weekends and holidays by the public, for gymnastics and almost every kind of indoor and outdoor sport, a range which stretches from badminton and basket ball to swimming and squash. It is no longer unique because there are now several other similar sports centres in a county that has been exceptionally quick to meet the challenge of increasing leisure.

There is quite an odour of sanctity about the Vale. Even if we omit the unfortunate Abbot, a mere bird of passage, it nurtured two Archbishops of Canterbury, Thomas Secker, a native of Sibthorpe, and Thomas Cranmer. Archbishop Cranmer (1489–1556) was born at Aslockton, a sprawling village just off the A52 east of Bingham, and spent his first 14 years there. The village pub is inevitably called the

Cranmer Arms, and the mound of a twelfth-century motte-and-bailey castle equally inevitably appears on the map as Cranmer's Mound. Aslockton Church is late-Victorian and uninteresting, but the Cranmers worshipped in Whatton Church, half a mile away across the little River Smite. In 1957 a chapel was restored in the Archbishop's memory in the church where his father is buried. The rest of the church was heavily restored in the nineteenth century, but there is good stained glass in the east window of the south aisle designed by Burne-Jones and executed by William Morris. Whatton village is a large, attractive agricultural centre with a school built in 1868 with material from an old dovecote in the grounds of Whatton Manor.

Another dovecote at Scarrington, just north of Aslockton, has been converted into a garage in the farmyard of the manor house, but an even more curious feature of this charming village is the mound of horseshoes outside the smithy. Mr George Flinders, the blacksmith, began the pile in 1945, intending to sell the shoes for scrap, but changed his mind when it became a local landmark. The pile now exceeds 16 feet and contains more than 50,000 shoes.

Between Scarrington and the Fosse Way is Car Colston. If I had to choose the most beautiful village in the county, I suppose that this—after much heart-searching—would be my choice. Having annoyed the inhabitants of many other places with strong claims to the title, I must now add further fuel to the fires by saying that Car Colston—red pantiles apart—is not a typical Nottinghamshire village at all. Cricket on the village green just does not happen much in the East Midlands. But it does at Car Colston. Come to that, large village greens are rare in these parts. Car Colston has two, one at either end of the village. The large one, where cricket is played, is nearly 18 acres in extent and is fringed by delightful houses—including a lovely Queen Anne one with a shell porch—and a pub and the village stocks. The other green is a mere six acres, but quite delightful. Car Colston is the type of village that you run across in Surrey or Sussex; in the East Midlands it is most unexpected. Which is not to say that these southern villages are necessarily more attractive; just that they are usually quite different in character.

Car Colston church has one of those splendid chancels that were built just after the Black Death, with sedilia and piscina very like those at Hawton, particularly graceful altar rails and a glorious east window.

For local historians it is also something of a place of pilgrimage to the tomb of Dr Robert Thoroton (1623–78), whose pioneer history of Nottinghamshire was published in 1677. He was a medical doctor with antiquarian interests who lived in the village at Moryn Hall, now a farmhouse. The county's local history society, named after him, has placed a tablet to him in the church.

The Thoroton family originated from the tiny hamlet of that name on the Smite, moved to Screveton, where Robert was born, and then to Flintham Hall, all very close together. The birthplace, Kirketon Hall, was demolished in 1823, but the tomb of one of its earlier owners, Richard Whalley (died 1583), with his three wives and 25 children, is in the small church at Screveton, which also has a few good misericords and a large ironbound chest of the fifteenth century. The seventeenth-century priest's house at the east end of the churchyard is a good example of half-timber and herringbone brick construction.

Flintham is a larger, well-wooded village that was larger still before some late-eighteenth century demolition of houses to allow the Hall grounds to be extended to their present 200 acres. Generally this northern side of the Vale is a countryside of corn and cattle, though nearer to Newark the hedges take on a grey jaded look from the dust of gypsum workings, the only blot on an otherwise fair landscape. Such settlements as there are, are tiny, though usually with some feature of interest, such as the brick tower and primitive Norman tympanium of Hawksworth church, the Norman doorway in a nineteenth-century brick tower at Flawborough, the Easter Sepulchre (inferior to Hawton's), splendid chancel and isolated, conical roofed, medieval dovecote at Sibthorpe; the last three all perhaps linked with the college of priests that was established there in 1324. And between the villages, often proclaiming their antiquity as the Fosse Way does, by forming parish boundaries, are the dykes; Carr Dyke, Moor Dyke, Back Dyke, which, with the Devon, Smite and tiny Whipling irrigate the Vale.

From Flawborough, which has less than 50 inhabitants, a road runs southward along a narrow limestone ridge that seems much higher than its 120–130 ft and offers magnificent views of the Duke of Rutland's romantic Belvoir Castle on a much higher spur just across the Leicestershire border. A mile or two south of Flawborough a linking road from the Fosse Way crosses the Smite and climbs through Orston to form a junction at the top of the village. Orston attempted

35. *The old school, Bunny, built by Sir Thomas Parkyns in* 1700

36. *Bunny Hall, once the home of Sir Thomas Parkyns who was his own architect*

unsuccessfully to cash in on the spa boom of the eighteenth century but struck gold in another way in 1952 when a board of 1,500 gold and silver coins, hidden during the Civil War, were ploughed up in a field.

Buried treasure seems comparatively common in Nottinghamshire. A parish clerk of the next village, Elton, dug up 200 Henry II silver coins in the churchyard in 1780. The church itself was reduced in size in 1857 and with the manor house and an inn form the bulk of what is not so much a village as a pleasant tree-encircled oasis at the point where the ridge-road crosses the A52. The trees continue towards Sutton, a hamlet even smaller than Elton. It forms part of the parish of Granby, which lies between two road junctions and still wears the air of a market town. But this is an illusion. Its population has been declining for centuries and now barely tops 300. The market has gone and its church was cut down to size in 1777, but is still worth visiting for the mermaids and other designs on its bench-ends and for the eighteenth-century gravestones so elaborately carved by a local craftsman, Thomas Wood of Bingham.

After such a series of declining villages, Barnstone comes as a surprise; but not an entirely pleasant one. It is modern, utilitarian; a ribbon-built appendage to a large cement works that is an ugly smudge on a lovely landscape to the tourist and a welcome alternative source of employment for the residents in a prosperous agricultural area where, as elsewhere, machines are increasingly displacing men on the farms.

Barnstone is in the parish of Langar, the Battersby-on-the-Hill of *The Way of All Flesh*, by Samuel Butler, who was born in the Georgian rectory on 4 December 1834, and is oddly ignored in a county that rightly makes so much of Byron and Lawrence. In fairness to the people of Nottinghamshire, it must be accepted that the whole country tended to ignore Butler after his death in 1902. As George Bernard Shaw wrote: 'Really, the English do not deserve to have great men. They allowed Butler to die practically unknown.' An *Everyman's Biographical Dictionary of Literature*, published in 1910, dismisses him in six lines, but devotes three times the length to the seventeenth-century satirist of the same name. The reason for that, apart from the usual decline in interest that follows an author's death, was that he was an anti-Establishment man whose satire was still sharp enough to get under the skin of pre-war Britain. But now that the later-twentieth century

37. *Boots Factory, Beeston, near Nottingham, by Sir Owen William, 1932. This south front is 550 ft long*

has caught up with Butler and is reading him again, one would expect a county which thinks highly of some other anti-Establishment figures to make more of him. True, the county did not see much of him after he went to Shrewsbury School—where his grandfather, Dr Butler, had been so distinguished a headmaster—and he had painted an unhappy picture of the villagers of Langar, not least of its rector, his father. Perhaps a tablet in the church might smack of hypocrisy, but there should surely be some indication somewhere that Butler was born in the village.

But perhaps it is even more curious that Admiral Richard, Earl Howe, (1726–1799) warrants only a modest tablet on a wall of the church whose transepts are crammed with splendid monuments to other Howes of Lanagar and their predecessors the Scropes, as well as to three generations of Chaworths from nearby Wiverton Hall. He has, it is true, a more elaborate monument in St Paul's Cathedral, but one expects something more striking than a plain tablet in the church where he is buried.

'As undaunted as a rock and as silent', was Horace Walpole's comment on the victor of the Glorious First of June, in which he captured seven French ships of the line in the battle of Ushant. From one of them came the present colourful altar cloth richly embroidered in Italy in the sixteenth century. 'Black Dick', as he was known in the navy, was not the only famous Howe. His elder brother, from whom he inherited the Viscountcy, was killed at Ticonderoga in the American War of Independence, and his young brother, the general, commanded the British Army in America, with little success, from 1775 until he resigned in 1778. Earlier generations produced some notable sons too, though most of their battles were political. Two of them, both called Scrope Howe, are commemorated by busts in the church.

The monuments are the outstanding feature of a fine church that is often described as 'the cathedral of the Vale', especially now that they have been re-gilded in a recent restoration that, as at Wollaton, has seen the altar moved westward into the nave. Best of all is the magnificent four-poster free-standing alabaster monument to Thomas Lord Scrope (died 1609) and his wife. "The recumbent figures and the dwarf-like bearded kneeling son at the feet of his parents", are, as Pevsner says, 'good enough to be Westminster Abbey'.

Wiverton, the former home of the Chaworths, lies two miles to the north. Jack Musters, Mary Chaworth's husband, built the present castellated mansion in 1814 (because of the hunting, of course) on the site of the former fortified manor house that was garrisoned for the Royalists and destroyed in 1645, except for the surviving gatehouse. There are no Chaworths there now. Nor is there either church or village. They disappeared long ago, as 'the necessary consequence of inclosure of good land', as Thoroton euphemistically put in 1677. So there is really nothing much to see at Wiverton except a few humps in a field; and the history of the Vale of Belvoir symbolised in one glance round an empty countryside.

Kinoulton, where the road sweeps up the long village street, across the reedy Grantham Canal, and on to the Wolds, also lost a church, but for different reasons. In the 1790s the squire, the Earl of Gainsborough, deciding that the old church near the Fosse Way was too far from the heart of the village, built a new one alongside the canal, using for the fabric brick from a specially built brickyard that was never used again. Traces of this old brickyard survive near Kinoulton Gorse, as do a few good slate headstones in the old churchyard. Other gravestones, according to a local story that deserves to be true, were used by the village baker to line his oven, a misdemeanour that was exposed when a customer noticed that his loaf bore the imprint of the words 'In loving memory'.

The history of the Nottinghamshire Wolds is not unlike that of the Vale of Belvoir, but with a twist at the end. It is a story of depopulation, with sheep-runs displacing cottages; the usual wold story, in fact. Thirty years ago, one could have left it at that. But now the people are coming back, especially on the edges of the Wolds, within commuting distance of Nottingham and Loughborough. Places like Keyworth and Plumtree, on the east, and West Leake, on the west, have grown rapidly recently, and even farther south, where the villages are more widely spaced, in-filling has brought new life to settlements that seemed in danger of becoming moribund. But, if the villages are generally bigger than those of the Vale, and there are signs of civilisation setting in, this still feels empty country; basically an open, breezy grassland plateau but cut through in places by brooks, generally running westward to Soar or Trent, so that it is often broken into a series of short steep hills and valleys that seem quite dramatic without ever much exceeding 350 ft or falling below 200 ft.

The obvious way, I suppose, to explore the Wolds from Kinoulton would be to use the various east-west minor roads, but I would prefer to turn north-westward, after crossing the Fosse, and head towards Nottingham on the fast Melton Mowbray-Nottingham road (A606T) that bypasses the villages, turning westward to Ruddington just short of Edwalton. This way you see, between the two villages, the magnificent rose gardens of that outstanding rose grower and character, Harry Wheatcroft, and approach Ruddington across the Nottingham-Loughborough road, so avoiding the trap of skirting its edge on the main road and thinking you have seen it.

There are many more beautiful villages in Nottinghamshire than Ruddington, but few more interesting. What at a casual glance could be mistaken for a soulless, overgrown commuter village turns out to be very much a place with a soul. It has an extraordinarily well-developed community sense. What other village of 6,000 inhabitants can produce a village booklet—issued free to every house? Not the usual pious account of the minutiae of the church's architecture, nor dull details about the product of a penny rate—though the information is there for those who want it—but a well produced, well written, splendidly illustrated, informative account of Ruddington's past, present and future. Among other items it contains information about village organizations, which number an astonishing 44.

The one that will most likely catch your eye is the Ruddington Framework Knitters' Shops Preservation Trust, which has bought two stockingers' shops and cottages and is setting up an industrial museum of the industry that caused the village's nineteenth-century growth. Closely allied to the Trust is the Local History Society, which supports a village museum, open by arrangement, and whose archaeological section is excavating the parish's mother church in the 'lost' village of Flawford. The church was demolished in 1773, and nothing remained but a few slate headstones in a jungle of long grass when the County Council decided in 1967 to clear it for a picnic area. The excavations that began then have revealed evidence of a Roman villa and a Saxon church from which the medieval building evolved. Ruddington's present parish church is unexciting in a late-Victorian urban style, but it seems to fit quite neatly into a village centre—with a village green redesigned in 1964—that is rightly a conservation area.

The last vestige of Nottingham commuterland fades away as the main road skirts Ruddington—with the merest hint of it at Bunny, a good way farther south. Bradmore lies off the main road; a small village with impressively large farm buildings. Most of the houses were destroyed in an early eighteenth-century fire and rebuilt immediately afterwards. Among the survivors was a good brick house with mullioned windows from the previous century, and the medieval church tower that has lost its church and is now attached to a small brick building.

Bunny is as delightful as its name. Much of the credit for that must go to Sir Thomas Parkyns (1663–1741) one of the most colourful and beneficent of Nottinghamshire's numerous eccentric squires. His monument is the most striking—almost literally—of several good Parkyns monuments in a particularly large and handsome, mainly fourteenth-century, church. It is a life-size representation of a powerful, stocky man with legs apart and knees slightly bent as though bracing himself against some impact, the hands thrust forward from bent elbows, with palms outstretched and turned inwards like a man helping his wife to wind her knitting wool; a smaller figure lies on a mat at the feet of Father Time. The mat is the clue. Sir Thomas is not knitting but wrestling.

Wrestling was his greatest interest. He wrote a book on *Cornish Hugg Wrestling*, in which he explained the mysteries of such esoteric holds as the 'back clamp', the 'gripe' and the 'hanging trippet'. He laid down strict rules about keeping fit, advising his readers to 'avoid being overtaken by drink, which very much enervates', and added that 'none but beef-eaters will go down with me, who have robust, healthy and sound bodies'.

But Sir Thomas was no mere theorist. He was a most enthusiastic performer who kept two professionals at Bunny Hall to wrestle with him, or with some promising young man whom he had found in one of his talent-hunting expeditions. To encourage local talent he instituted an annual wrestling tournament at Bunny, offering a lace hat worth 22 shillings as first prize, thus also encouraging local industry. When the tournament was last held, in 1810, two years short of its centenary, Sir Thomas had been in his coffin for nearly 70 years.

It was, naturally, a stone coffin, as the collecting of stone coffins was one of his more off-beat hobbies, and he elected to be buried in his most choice piece, the more commonplace exhibits being given to his tenants, whose need for them had been delayed by the health service he ran for their benefit and to keep his own knowledge of medicine in trim. He may also have given free legal aid, since he had practised law as a young man.

He certainly built them houses and a school; not simply paying for them but designing them as well. Bradmore was rebuilt to his design and some of the best buildings in Bunny are his. The old school—now used as a village hall—is perhaps the best. With its steep-pitched roof, quoins and small mullioned windows it looks a century older than the 1700 that appears on a date-stone. Along the string course dividing ground floor from the first floor is a Latin inscription translated as: 'Learning has no enemy except ignorance.'

Opposite, behind a wall said to be three miles in extent and to have taken three years to build (a mile a year seems to have been the traditional Nottinghamshire speed), is Bunny Hall, where he lived and wrote a Latin Grammar as well as his wrestling book. He designed it himself, of course, and the result is a decidedly unconventional house, now used as flats, that really defies description.

At the southern end of the village the road crosses Fairham Brook and climbs steeply up Bunny Hill on to the Wolds proper. To the left, Old Wood is carpeted with bluebells in spring, and beyond that is Windmill Hill, afforested by Lord Rancliffe, a later Parkyns and a great tree planter.

The next place, Costock, is a cross-roads village looking remarkably like Granby, but with more signs of reviving life. Its fine stone-built Elizabethan manor house is not easy to see from the road.

The road going westward from Costock follows the valley of another brook to East Leake, which has recently been submerged by subtopia, and West Leake, which so far has managed to keep the twentieth century at arm's length. Northward, across some pretty, tumbled country, marred by large gypsum mines, lies Gotham, which has not much to commend it except the often-told tales of its 'wise men' whose numerous exploits included planting a hedge around a cuckoo, and raking a pool to rescue the moon reflected in it. Such tales are told of other English villages, but Gotham has had most of the publicity. A shawm, or vamping horn, in East Leake church was used to 'vamp' the singing until 1855, and is one of only six left in England. This, and the odd stretches of pleasant country excepting, is an avoidable corner of the Wolds.

On the whole, it is better to continue along the main road to Rempstone, of which Cecil Roberts, another Nottingham-born writer, has written with affection. The church, dating from 1773 and one of the best examples of that period in the county, is surprisingly cut off by the main road from the rest of the village, which lies east of the A60, and contains one of the most fearsome bends in the Midlands. But to compensate for the shock of turning about 105 degrees round the wall of a house, there are some attractive houses, including one thatched cottage, with colourful olde worlde garden to match, that might have jumped straight out of a British Travel poster.

East of Rempstone, which has a popular traction-engine rally in high summer, are the 'W' villages; Wysall, Widmerpool and Willoughby-on-the-Wolds. All are attractive brick villages with the usual pantile roofs, but Widmerpool has a well-wooded park round a Victorian neo-Elizabethan house that is not open to the public, Wysall and Willoughby are open and wind-swept; unmistakably wold villages.

The last Civil War battle on Nottinghamshire soil was fought at Willoughby in July 1648. It was a sharp engagement in which the victorious Cromwellians lost 30 men and the Royalists '44 gentlemen of quality', including Colonel Michael Stanhope, of the Shelford family, who is commemorated in the church by a small brass. But this is of minor interest compared with the elegant effigies of medieval Willoughbys, the earliest in stone, the later in alabaster, which are some of the best monuments in the county.

From Willoughby-on-the-Wolds a long, lonely road crosses the Fosse Way near the site of the Roman station of *Vernemetum* and continues to Upper Broughton, which stands high and isolated in the extreme south-eastern tip of Nottinghamshire. A long and attractive village street leads to a small green on which stands a cross reputedly commemorating deliverance from the Black Death. Near it is a lead cistern of 1777 carved with the signs of the Zodiac. Beyond the green the small church in crumbling amber sandstone is separated from the village street by the Nottingham-Melton road, which winds round a series of sinuous bends and drops sharply down to a narrow bridge over a brook that marks the county boundary, and then climbs even more steeply away into Leicestershire.

Index

Index